contents

P9-EJZ-833

Check It Out!

Turn to the inside back cover to find abbreviations,
an explanation of skill levels, and even a handy ruler!

let's go on a yarn shop hop

You've loved the other books in our 60 Quick Knits series, and now we're delighted to bring you *60 Quick Knits from America's Yarn Shops*, a unique collection of favorite patterns from yarn shops across the country—maybe even yours!

We invited shops to share popular designs by owners, employees, and customers, and the result is an amazing assortment of time-tested knits, from accessories to baby items to home décor—something for every style and skill level. The patterns all use yarns from the Cascade 220 and 220 Superwash lines, which are soft, durable, and affordable, with an unmatchable range of solid and variegated colors.

The dozens of projects in this book combine the best of two worlds: America's favorite yarns and America's favorite yarn shops!

To locate retailers that carry Cascade 220 and 220 Superwash, visit cascadeyarns.com.

Slouchy Lace Hat

A little slouch and a lot of lace are a pretty combination for a sweet topper.

DESIGNED BY ANDREA PANZICA, KNITTERS MERCANTILE, COLUMBUS, OH

Size
Woman's Medium

Knitted Measurements
Brim circumference 20"/51cm
Length 10½"/27cm

Materials
■ 1 3½oz/100g hank (each approx 220yd/201m) of Cascade Yarns *Cascade 220 Heathers* (wool) in #2419 aster

■ Size 5 (3.75mm) circular needle, 16"/40cm long, *or size to obtain gauge*

■ Size 4 (3.5mm) circular needle, 16"/40cm long

■ One set (5) size 5 (3.75mm) double-pointed needles (dpns)

■ Stitch markers

Hat
With larger circular needle, cast on 110 sts. Join to work in the rnd, taking care not to twist sts, and place marker (pm) for beg of rnd.
Rnds 1 and 2 [P11, pm] 10 times.
Rnd 3 *[K2tog] twice, [yo, k1] three times, yo, [SKP] twice; rep from * around.

Rnd 4 Knit.
Change to smaller needle.
Rnd 5 Purl.
Rnds 6–15 *P2, k2, p2, k1, p2, k2; rep from * around.
Rnd 16 Purl.
Change to larger circular needle.
Rnd 17 *[K2tog] twice, [yo, k1] three times, yo, [SKP] twice; rep from * around.
Rnd 18 Knit.
Rnd 19 *[K2tog] twice, [yo, k1] three times, yo, [SKP] twice; rep from * around.
Rnd 20 *P1, k9, p1; rep from * around.
Rnd 21 Knit.
Rnd 22 *P1, k9, p1; rep from * around.
Rnds 23 and 24 Knit.
Rnd 25 *K3, p5, k3; rep from * around.
Rnds 26 and 27 Knit.
Rnd 28 Purl.
Rep rnds 17–28 three times more.

CROWN SHAPING
Note Change to dpns (dividing sts evenly among 4 needles) when there are too few sts on circular needle.
Rnd 1 *[K2tog] twice, [yo, k1] three times, yo, [SKP] twice; rep from * around.
Rnd 2 Knit.
Rnd 3 *[K2tog] twice, [yo, k1] three times, yo, [SKP] twice; rep from * around.
Rnd 4 *P2tog, k8, p2, k8, p2tog; rep from * around—100 sts.

Rnd 5 Knit.
Rnd 6 *P2tog, k7, p2, k7, p2tog; rep from * around—90 sts.
Rnd 7 Knit.
Rnd 8 *K2tog, k14, ssk; rep from * around—80 sts.
Rnd 9 Knit.
Rnd 10 *K2tog, k12, ssk; rep from * around—70 sts.
Rnd 11 Purl.
Rnd 12 *K2tog, yo, k1, yo, [SKP] twice, [k2tog] twice, yo, k1, yo, ssk; rep from * around—60 sts.
Rnd 13 Knit.
Rnd 14 *K2tog, yo, [SKP] twice, [k2tog] twice, yo, ssk; rep from * around—40 sts.
Rnd 15 *P1, k2, p2, k2, p1; rep from * around.
Rnd 16 *K2tog, k4, ssk; rep from * around—30 sts.
Rnd 17 *P1, k1, p2, k1, p1; rep from * around.
Rnd 18 *K2tog, k2, ssk; rep from * around—20 sts.
Break yarn, leaving 10"/25cm tail. Thread tail through rem sts. Pull tightly to secure.

Finishing
Block lightly to measurements. ■

Gauge
22 sts and 26 rows to 4"/10cm over pat st using size 5 (3.75mm) needles. *Take time to check gauge.*

Cable Hearts Capelet

Creatively arranged cables form a ring of hearts around the bottom of a sweet wrap.

DESIGNED BY TINA JOHNSTON, BLACK SHEEP AT ORENCO, HILLSBORO, OR

■■□□

Knitted Measurements
Circumference 36"/91.5cm
Height 6½"/16.5cm

Materials
■ 1 3½oz/100g hank (each approx 220yd/201m) of Cascade Yarns *Cascade 220* in #9422 Tibetan rose
■ Size 8 (5mm) circular needle, 24"/61cm long, *or size to obtain gauge*
■ Cable needle (cn)

Stitch Glossary
6-st LC Sl 3 sts to cn, hold to *front*, k3, k3 from cn.
4-st RC Sl 2 sts to cn, hold to *back*, k2, k2 from cn.
3-st RC Sl 1 st to cn, hold to *back*, k2, k1 from cn.
3-st LC Sl 2 sts to cn, hold to *front*, k1, k2 from cn.
RT K2tog, leave sts on needle, then insert RH needle between 2 sts just knitted tog and k the first st again, then sl both sts from LH needle.

Note
The 6-st cables at the end of rows 10 and 16 are worked with the last 3 sts of the round and the 1st 3 sts of the following rnd.

Capelet
Cast on 180 sts loosely. Join to work in the rnd, being careful not to twist sts, and place marker (pm) for beg of rnd.
Rnds 1–3 *K6, p6; rep from * to end of rnd.
Rnd 4 P3, *6-st LC, p6; rep from * to last 3 sts, p3.
Rnd 5 P3, k6, *p6, k6; rep from * to last 3 sts, p3.
Rnd 6 P2, *3-st RC, p2, 3-st LC, p4; rep from * to last 10 sts, 3-st RC, p2, 3-st LC, p2.
Rnd 7 P2, *k3, p2, k3, p4; rep from * to last 10 sts, k3, p2, k3, p2.
Rnd 8 P1, 3-st RC, p4, *3-st LC, p2, 3-st RC, p4; rep from * to last 4 sts, 3-st LC, p1.
Rnd 9 P1, k3, p4, k3, *p2, k3, p4, k3; rep from * to last st, p1.
Rnd 10 P1, k2, p6, *6-st LC, p6; rep from * to last 3 sts, 6-st LC, replacing marker in center of cable.

Rnd 11 Begin after cable: p6, *k6, p6; rep from * to last 3 sts, k3.
Rnd 12 P1, 3-st RC, *p1, k2, p1, 3-st LC, p2, 3-st RC; rep from * to last 8 sts, p1, k2, p1, 3-st LC, p1.
Rnd 13 P1, k3, p1, RT, p1, *k3, p2, k3, p1, RT, p1; rep from * to last 4 sts, k1, p1.
Rnd 14 Rep row 12.
Rnd 15 P1, k4, RT, *k4, p2, k4, RT, rep from * to last 5 sts, k1, p1.
Rnd 16 P1, k2, *p2, k2, p2, 6-st LC; rep from * to end of rnd, replacing marker in center of final cable.
Rnd 17 P4, k4, *p8, k4; rep from * to last 4 sts, p4.
Rnd 18 P4, *4-st RC, p8; rep from * to last 8 sts, 4-st RC, p4.
Rnd 19 Rep row 17.
Rnds 20–23 P3, *k2, p2, k2, p6; rep from * to last 9 sts, k2, p2, k2, p3.
Rnds 24–42 Rep rows 17–23 twice more, then rows 17–21 once more.
Rnd 43 P3, k6, *p6, k6; rep from * to last 3 sts, p3.
Bind off.

Finishing
Block lightly to measurements. ■

Gauge
18 sts and 24 rows to 4"/10cm over St st using size 8 (5mm) needles.
Take time to check gauge.

Garter Lace Striped Shawl

A garter stitch triangle is taken to another level with lacy stripes at the bottom and pretty picot around the edges.

DESIGNED BY CHARLENE HATFIELD, STITCH IN TIME, HOWELL, MI

Knitted Measurements
Height at center 18"/45.5cm
Width at top 70"/177.5cm

Materials
- 1 3½oz/100g hank (each approx 220yd/201m) of Cascade Yarns *Cascade 220* (wool) each in #7815 summer sky (A), #8339 marine (B), and #2404 Atlantic (C)
- One pair size 10 (6mm) needles *or size to obtain gauge*

Stitch Glossary
Kfb Knit into the front and back of next st—1 st increased.
Pfb Purl into the front and back of next st—1 st increased.

Window Lace Pattern
Rows 1 and 3 (WS) Knit.
Row 2 Purl.
Row 4 P3, *yo, k1, yo, p3; rep from * to end.
Rows 5, 7, and 9 K3, *p3, k3; rep from * to end.
Rows 6 and 8 P3, *yo, k3tog, yo, p3; rep from * to end.
Row 10 P3, *k3tog, p3; rep from * to end.
Rep rows 1–10 for window lace pat.

Horseshoe Lace Pattern
Row 1 (RS) Yo, k4, sl 1, k2tog, psso, k4, yo, k1, *yo, k4, sl 1, k2tog, psso, k4, yo, k1; rep from * to last 15 sts, yo, k4, sl 1, k2tog, psso, k4, yo, k4.
Row 2 and all even-numbered rows Knit.
Row 3 K5, yo, k3, sl 1, k2tog, psso, k3, yo, k2, *k1, yo, k3, sl 1, k2tog, psso, k3, yo, k2; rep from * to last 15 sts, k1, yo, k3, sl 1, k2tog, psso, k3, yo, k5.

Row 5 K6, yo, k2, sl 1, k2tog, psso, k2, yo, k3, *k2, yo, k2, sl 1, k2tog, psso, k2, yo, k3; rep from * to last 15 sts, k2, yo, k2, sl 1, k2tog, psso, k2, yo, k6.
Row 7 K7, yo, k1, sl 1, k2tog, psso, k1, yo, k4, *k3, yo, k1, sl 1, k2tog, psso, k1, yo, k4; rep from * to last 15 sts, k3, yo, k1, sl 1, k2tog, psso, k1, yo, k7.
Row 9 K8, yo, sl 1, k2tog, psso, yo, k5, *k4, yo, sl 1, k2tog, psso, yo, k5; rep from * to last 15 sts, k4, yo, sl 1, k2tog, psso, yo, k8.
Rep rows 1–9 for horseshoe lace pat.

Shawl
With A, cast on 11 sts.
Row 1 K1, p1, k7, p1, k1.
Row 2 and all even-numbered rows Kfb, knit to last st, kfb.
Row 3 Kfb, k1, yo, p1, k7, p1, yo, k1, kfb—17 sts.
Row 5 Kfb, k4, yo, p1, k7, p1, yo, k4, kfb—23 sts.
Row 7 Kfb, k7, yo, p1, k7, p1, yo, k7, kfb—29 sts.
Row 9 Kfb, k10, yo, p1, k7, p1, yo, k10, kfb—35 sts.
Row 11 Kfb, k13, yo, p1, k7, p1, yo, k13, kfb—41 sts.

Gauge
12 sts and 19 rows to 4"/10cm over garter st (k every row) using size 10 (6mm) needles.
Take time to check gauge.

Garter Lace Striped Shawl

Row 13 Kfb, k16, yo, p1, k7, p1, yo, k16, kfb—47 sts.
Row 15 Kfb, k19, yo, p1, k7, p1, yo, k19, kfb—53 sts.
Row 17 Kfb, k22, yo, p1, k7, p1, yo, k22, kfb—59 sts.
Row 19 Kfb, k25, yo, p1, k7, p1, yo, k25, kfb—65 sts.
Row 21 Kfb, k28, yo, p1, k7, p1, yo, k28, kfb—71 sts.
Row 23 Kfb, k31, yo, p1, k7, p1, yo, k31, kfb—77 sts.
Row 25 Kfb, k34, yo, p1, k2, p1, yo, k34, kfb—83 sts.
Row 27 Kfb, k37, yo, p1, k2, p1, yo, k37, kfb—89 sts.
Row 29 Kfb, k40, yo, p1, k2, p1, yo, k40, kfb—95 sts.
Row 31 Kfb, k43, yo, p1, k2, p1, yo, k43, kfb—101 sts.
Row 33 Kfb, k46, yo, p1, k2, p1, yo, k46, kfb—107 sts.
Row 35 Kfb, k49, yo, p1, k2, p1, yo, k49, kfb—113 sts.
Row 37 Kfb, k52, yo, p1, k2, p1, yo, k52, kfb—119 sts.
Row 39 Kfb, k55, yo, p1, k2, p1, yo, k55, kfb—125 sts.
Row 41 Kfb, k58, yo, p1, k2, p1, yo, k58, kfb—131 sts.
Row 43 Kfb, k61, yo, p1, k2, p1, yo, k61, kfb—137 sts.
Row 45 Kfb, k64, yo, p1, k2, p1, yo, k64, kfb—143 sts.
Row 47 Kfb, k67, yo, p1, k2, p1, yo, k67, kfb—149 sts.
Row 49 Kfb, k70, yo, p1, k2, p1, yo, k70, kfb—155 sts.
Row 51 Kfb, k73, yo, p1, k2, p1, yo, k73, kfb—161 sts.
Row 53 Kfb, k76, yo, p1, k2, p1, yo, k76, kfb—167 sts.

Row 55 Kfb, k79, yo, p1, k2, p1, yo, k79, kfb—173 sts.
Row 57 Kfb, k82, yo, p1, k2, p1, yo, k82, kfb—179 sts.
Row 59 Kfb, k85, yo, p1, k2, p1, yo, k85, kfb—185 sts.
Row 60 Kfb, knit to last st, kfb—187 sts.

BEG WINDOW LACE PAT
Row 1 With B, work row 1 of window lace pat, AT THE SAME TIME, kfb in first 2 sts and last 2 sts—191 sts.
Row 2 Work row 2 of window lace pat, AT THE SAME TIME, pfb in first 2 sts and last 2 sts—195 sts.
Work rows 3–10 of window lace pat.
Knit 1 row.
Next row (RS) With C, knit, inc 16 sts evenly across—211 sts.
Knit 1 row.
Work horseshoe lace pat for 10 rows.
Knit 2 rows, kfb in first and last st of each row—311 sts.
Next row (RS) *K2tog, yo; rep from * to last st, k1—311 sts.
Knit 2 rows, kfb in first and last st of each row—315 sts.
Knit 1 row.
Next row (WS) *Cast on 1, bind off 3; rep from * to end.

Finishing
PICOT EDGING
With C, pick up approx 304 sts evenly along sides and top edge.
Next row *Cast on 1, bind off 3; rep from * to end.
Block lightly to measurements. ■

Flowered Headband

Soft colors and a knitted flower make a feminine accessory just right for springtime.

DESIGNED BY SANDY PAYNE, DEBBIE MACOMBER'S A GOOD YARN SHOP, PORT ORCHARD, WA

Size
Woman's Medium

Knitted Measurements
Brim circumference (unstretched)
16"/40.5cm
Width 4"/10cm

Materials
■ 1 1¾oz/50g hank (each approx 164yd/150m) of Cascade Yarns *Cascade 220 Sport* (wool) each in #9602 soft sage (MC) and #9593 ginseng (CC)

■ One pair each sizes 3, 5, and 8 (3.25, 3.75, and 5mm) needles *or size to obtain gauge*

Note
Slip first stitch of every row purlwise, with yarn in front.

Headband
With size 5 (3.75mm) needles and MC, cast on 23 sts.
Rows 1–6 Sl 1, k to end of row.
Row 7 (RS) Sl 1, k9, yo, k3, yo, k10—25 sts.
Row 8 Sl 1, k8, p7, k9.
Row 9 Sl 1, k10, SK2P, k11—23 sts.
Row 10 Sl 1, k8, p5, k9.
Rep rows 7–10 three times more, then rows 7–9 once.
Row 26 Sl 1, k to end of row.
Rep rows 1–26 five times more, then rows 1–6 once. Bind off.

Finishing
Sew bound-off and cast-on edges together. Gather seam.

LARGE FLOWER (MAKE 1)
With size 8 (5mm) needles and CC, cast on 63 stitches. Change to size 3 (3.25mm) needles.
Row 1 (RS) Knit.
Row 2 and all WS rows Purl.
Row 3 *K5, k2tog; rep from * to end of row—54 sts.
Row 5 *K4, k2tog; rep from * to end of row—45 sts.

Row 7 *K3, k2tog; rep from * to end of row—36 sts.
Row 9 *K2tog; rep from * to end of row—18 sts.
Row 11 Knit.
Break yarn, leaving a long tail. Thread yarn through rem sts and gather tightly to secure. Sew side edges together. Sew flower to headband, centering on headband seam.

SMALL FLOWER (MAKE 1)
With size 8 (5mm) needles and CC, cast on 49 stitches. Change to size 3 (3.25mm) needles.
Row 1 (RS) Knit.
Row 2 and all WS rows Purl.
Row 3 *K5, k2tog; rep from * to end of row—42 sts.
Row 5 *K4, k2tog; rep from * to end of row—35 sts.
Row 7 *K3, k2tog; rep from * to end of row—28 sts.
Row 9 *K2tog; rep from * to end of row—14 sts.
Row 11 Knit.
Break yarn, leaving a long tail. Thread yarn through rem sts and gather tightly to secure. Sew side edges together. Center small flower over large flower and secure. ■

Gauge
22 sts and 40 rows to 4"/10cm over St st using size 5 (3.75mm) needles.
Take time to check gauge.

Cable Cuff Mittens

A striking woven cable circles the wrist, knit in a solid to complement the variegated main color.

DESIGNED BY MEGHAN JONES, PARADISE FIBERS, SPOKANE, WA

Knitted Measurements
Hand circumference 7½"/19cm
Length 10¼"/26cm

Materials
■ 1 3½oz/100g hank (each approx 220yd/201m) of Cascade Yarns *Cascade 220 Paints* (wool) in #9923 denim storm (MC)

■ 1 3½oz/100g hank (each approx 220yd/201m) of Cascade Yarns *Cascade 220* (wool) in #8509 grey (CC)

■ One set (5) size 7 (4.5mm) double-pointed needles (dpns) *or size to obtain gauge*

■ Stitch markers

■ Cable needle (cn)

■ Stitch holders

■ Tapestry needle

Note
The cuff is knit flat and seamed together, and the main hand is picked up and knit from the side of the cuff.

Stitch Glossary
4-st LC Sl 2 sts to cn and hold to *front*, k2, k2 from cn.
4-st RC Sl 2 sts to cn and hold to *back*, k2, k2 from cn.

Woven Cable Panel
(over 20 sts)
Row 1 K1, k2, p2, 4-st LC, 4-st LC, k2, p2, k2, k1.
Rows 2 and 4 K1, p2, k2, p10, k2, p2, k1.
Row 3 K1, k2, p2, k2, 4-st RC, 4-st RC, p2, k2, k1.
Rep rows 1–4 for woven cable panel.

Stripe Sequence
Rnd 1 With CC, knit.
Rnd 2 With CC, sl 1, knit to end of rnd.
Rnd 3 With MC, knit.
Rnd 4 With MC, sl 1, knit to end of rnd.
Rnds 5–8 Rep rnds 1–4.
Rnd 9 With CC, knit.
Rnd 10 With MC, sl 1, knit to end of rnd.

Mitten (make 2)
CUFF
Using CC, cast on 20 sts. Rep rows 1–4 of woven cable panel until piece measures 7½"/19cm from cast-on edge, ending with a RS row. Bind off all stitches on WS. Graft cast-on edge and bound-off edge tog.

Hand
Using MC and beg at seam, pick up and k 36 sts evenly around one edge of cuff (approx 2 sts for every 3 rows). Join to work in the rnd and place marker (pm) for beg of rnd.

GUSSET
Set-up rnd K26, pm, k1, pm, k to end.
Rnd 1 (inc) Knit to m, sm, M1L, knit to m, M1R, sm, knit to end.
Rnds 2 and 3 Knit.
Rep rnds 1–3 five times more—48 sts. Work even until piece measures 2½"/6.5cm from picked-up sts.
Next rnd Knit to 1st marker, remove marker, place foll 13 sts onto holder, cast on 2 sts, sl m, k to end—37 sts.
Next rnd Knit.
Next rnd (dec) K to 2 sts before marker, k2tog, remove marker, k to end—36 sts. Join CC and work 10-row stripe sequence once.

Gauge
19 sts and 27 rnds to 4"/10cm over St st using size 7 (4.5mm) needles.
Take time to check gauge.

Cable Cuff Mittens

Break CC and cont in St st with MC until piece measures 6"/15.cm, or 1½"/4cm shorter than desired length, from picked-up sts.

TOP SHAPING
Rnd 1 *K4, k2tog; rep from * to end of rnd—30 sts.
Rnds 2 and 3 Knit.
Rnd 4 *K3, k2tog; rep from * to end of rnd—24 sts.
Rnds 5 and 6 Knit.
Rnd 7 *K2, k2tog; rep from * to end of rnd—18 sts.
Rnd 8 Knit.
Rnd 9 *K1, k2tog; rep from * to end of rnd—12 sts.
Rnd 10 *K2tog; rep from * to end of rnd—6 sts.
Break yarn, leaving 6"/15cm tail. Thread through rem sts, pull tightly to secure.

Thumb
Place 13 sts on holder onto dpns.
Rnd 1 With MC, pick up and k 4 sts across gap, pm, knit to end of rnd—17 sts.
Rnd 2 Knit.
Rnd 3 Knit to last 4 sts, [k2tog] twice—15 sts.
Work even in St st until piece measures 2"/5cm.

TOP SHAPING
Rnd 1 *K3, k2tog; rep from * to end of rnd—12 sts.
Rnd 2 Knit.
Rnd 3 *K2tog; rep from * to end of rnd—6 sts.
Break yarn, leaving 6"/15cm tail. Thread through rem sts, pull tightly to secure.

Finishing
BORDER
Using MC and dpns, cast on 3 sts. Do not turn work. Slide sts to right end of needle and hold yarn at back.
Row 1 *K2, sl 1 knitwise wyib; starting at seam with WS facing, pick up and k 1 st at edge of cuff, pass slipped st over picked-up st, do not turn work. Slide sts to other end of needle; rep from *, picking up 2 sts for every 3 rows, to end. Bind off 3 sts, sew bound-off to cast-on edge.
Block lightly to measurements. ∎

Fair Isle Bonnet

You'll be ready for the Easter parade in this pastel-pretty Fair Isle creation with a soft brim.

DESIGNED BY SUSAN GRESSMAN, HILL CREEK YARN SHOPPE, COLUMBUS, MO

Size
Woman's Large

Knitted Measurements
Circumference (excluding brim)
26"/ 66cm
Length (including brim) 9"/ 23cm

Materials
■ 1 1¾oz/50g hank (each approx 273yd/250m) of Cascade Yarns *Cascade 220 Fingering* (wool) each in #9592 sage (A), #9595 dark periwinkle (B), #9594 orchid haze (C), and #9421 blue Hawaii (D)

■ Size 5 (3.75mm) circular needle, 16"/40.5cm long, *or size to obtain gauge*

■ One set (5) size 5 (3.75mm) double-pointed needles (dpns)

■ Stitch markers

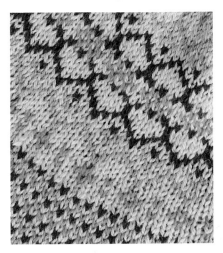

Stitch Glossary
CDD (centered double decrease)
Sl 2 tog knitwise, k1, psso.
Kfb Knit into the front and back of next st—1 st increased.

I-Cord Cast-on
Cast on 3 sts. Slide sts purlwise back to left needle. *Kfb, k2, slide 3 sts purlwise back to left needle, leaving one st on right needle; rep from * until desired number of sts have been cast on (count the three I-cord sts as part of the cast-on sts).

Hat
With circular needle and A, cast on 196 sts using I-cord cast-on. Join to work in the rnd, taking care not to twist sts, and place marker for beg of rnd.
Work rnds 1–6 of chart 1 twice, then work rnd 1 once more (13 rnds total).
With A, work one rnd even.
Next rnd K2tog, *k2tog, k2; rep from * to last 2 sts, k2tog—146 sts.
Work rnds 1–34 of chart 2 as foll: *work 1st 6-st rep 10 times, work center section of chart, work 2nd 6-st rep 10 times. On rnd 35 of chart, dec 2 sts evenly around—144 sts.

CROWN SHAPING
Note Change to dpns when sts no longer comfortably fit on circular needle.
Work rnds 1–18 of chart 3—16 sts.
Next rnd [CDD, k1] four times—8 sts.
Break yarn, leaving 12"/30cm tail. Thread tail through rem sts. Pull tight and secure.

Finishing
Block lightly to measurements. ■

Gauge
26 sts and 32 rows to 4"/10cm over St st using size 5 (3.75mm) needles.
Take time to check gauge.

Fair Isle Bonnet

CHART 2

Color and Stitch Key

☐	Sage (A)
■	Dark periwinkle (B)
▨	Orchid haze (C)
▨	Blue Hawaii (D)
⋏	CDD
▨	No stitch

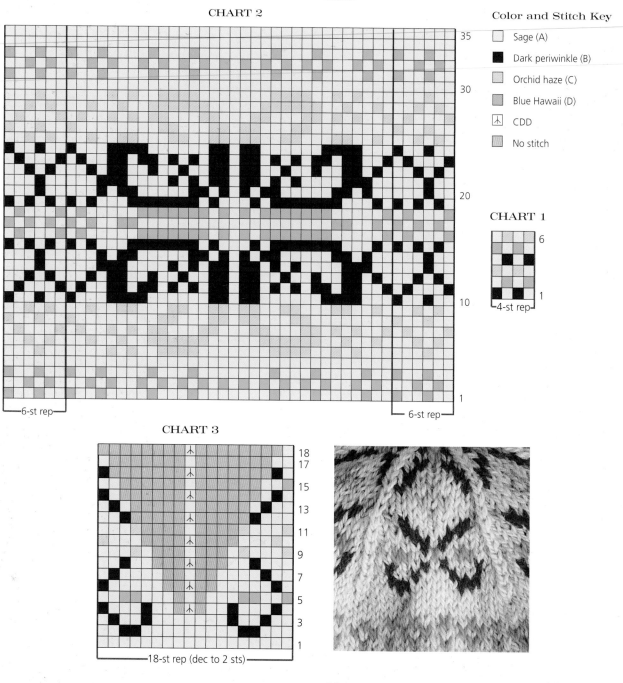

35

30

20

10

1

6-st rep

6-st rep

CHART 1

6

1

4-st rep

CHART 3

18
17
15
13
11
9
7
5
3
1

18-st rep (dec to 2 sts)

Twisted Rib Hat

An easy allover stitch pattern adds the perfect amount of texture to a comfortably slouchy shape.

DESIGNED BY TALITHA KUOMI, IN THE LOOP, PLAINVILLE, MA

Sizes
Instructions are written for Woman's Small. Changes for sizes Medium and Large are in parentheses.

Knitted Measurements
Brim circumference (stretched)
19 (21, 23)"/48 (53.5, 58.5)cm

Materials
■ 1 (1, 2) 3½oz/100g ball(s) (each approx 220yd/201m) of Cascade Yarns *220 Superwash* (superwash wool) in #848 blueberry

■ One each sizes 7 and 9 (4.5 and 5.5mm) circular needle, 16"/41cm long, *or size to obtain gauge*

■ Stitch markers

Stitch Glossary
K1-b Knit into next st and the st in the row below at the same time.

Twisted Rib
(multiple of 2 sts)
Rnd 1 *P1, k1 tbl; rep from * to marker, sl marker.
Rep rnd 1 for twisted rib.

Shaker Rib
(multiple of 2 sts)
Rnd 1 *P1, k1; rep from * around.
Rnd 2 *P1, k1-b; rep from * around.
Rep rnds 1 and 2 for shaker rib.

Hat
BRIM
Using smaller needle, cast on 100 (110, 120) sts.
Join to knit in the rnd, being careful not to twist sts, and place marker (pm) for beg of rnd.
Work in twisted rib until piece measures approx 2¼"/5.5cm.

BODY
Change to larger needle. Cont in shaker rib until piece measures approx 6¼"/16cm, ending with rnd 2.
Set-up rnd P1, k1, p1, pm, k2tog, work in shaker rib as est for 48 sts, ssk, pm, k1, p1, k1, pm, k2tog, work in shaker rib as est to last 2 sts, ssk.
Rnd 1 P1, k1-b, p1, sl marker, k1, work in shaker rib to last st before marker, p1, sl marker, k1-b, p1, k1-b, sl marker, p1, work in shaker rib to last st before marker, k1.
Rnd 2 (dec) P1, k1, p1, sl marker, k2tog, work in shaker rib to 2 sts before marker, ssk, sl marker, k1, p1, k1, sl marker,

Gauges
20 sts and 26 rows to 4"/10cm over St st using size 9 (5.5mm) needles.
28 sts and 28 rows to 4"/10cm over twisted rib using size 7 (4.5mm) needles.
18 sts and 23 rows to 4"/10cm over shaker rib using size 9 (5.5mm) needles. *Take time to check gauges.*

Twisted Rib Hat

k2tog, work in shaker rib to last 2 sts, ssk, sl marker.
Rep rnds 1 and 2 for 5 (7, 9) times more—76 (78, 80) sts.
Rep rnd 1 once.

CROWN SHAPING
Change to smaller needle.
Rnds 1 and 2 P1, k1 tbl, p1, sl marker, k1 tbl, work in twisted rib to 1 st before marker, k1 tbl, sl marker, k1 tbl, p1, k1 tbl, sl marker, k1 tbl, work in twisted rib to last st, k1 tbl, sl marker.
Rnd 3 (dec) P1, k1 tbl, p1, sl marker, k2tog tbl, work in twisted rib to 2 sts before marker, ssk, sl marker, k1 tbl, p1, k1 tbl, sl marker, k2tog tbl, work in twisted rib to last 2 sts, ssk, sl marker.
Rep rnds 1–3 two times more—64 (66, 68) sts.
Next rnd P2tog, p1, remove marker, k1 tbl, work in twisted rib to 1 st before marker, k1 tbl, remove marker, k2tog tbl, pm, k1 tbl, remove marker, k1 tbl, work in twisted rib to last st, k1 tbl, remove marker—62 (64, 66) sts.

Finishing

Remove beg-of-rnd marker. Sl 1 st purlwise from LH needle to RH needle. Slide 31 (32, 33) sts to one end of needle and rem 31 (32, 33) sts to other end of the needle, letting final marker divide the two sets of sts. Graft these live sts at top of crown closed, removing final marker. Sew both ends of this top seam tog at center top of hat. Block lightly to measurements. ∎

Bubble Hat

Pops of color are bursting out all over this bright and bubbly hat that's also extra warm.

DESIGNED BY DIANA JIMENEZ, THE YARN GARDEN, WHITTIER, CA

Size
Adult Medium

Knitted Measurements
Head circumference 22"/56cm
Depth 8½"/22cm

Materials
■ 1 1¾oz/50g hank (each approx 136yd/125m) of Cascade Yarns *220 Superwash Sport* (superwash merino) each in #854 navy (A), #1967 wisteria (B), #827 coral (C), and #1942 mint (D)

■ One each sizes 4 and 6 (3.5 and 4mm) circular needle, 16"/40cm long, *or size to obtain gauge*

■ One set (5) size 6 (4mm) double-pointed needles (dpns)

■ Stitch marker

■ Tapestry needle

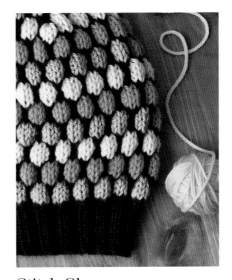

Stitch Glossary
K5b Drop next st off LH needle and unravel 4 rows. Insert tip of LH needle into the st in A, and then under all 4 loose strands with it. Knit tog, trapping loose strands behind st.

K2, P2 Rib
(multiple of 4 sts)
Rnd 1 *K2, p2, rep from * to end of rnd.
Rep rnd 1 for k2, p2 rib.

Gauges
22 sts and 29 rows to 4"/10cm over St st using size 6 (4mm) needles.
21 sts and 25 rows to 4"/10cm over bubble st pat using size 6 (4mm) needles.
Take time to check gauges.

Bubble Hat

Hat

With A and smaller circular needle, cast on 112 sts. Join, being careful not to twist sts, and place marker for beg of rnd. Work in k2, p2 rib for 1½"/4cm. Change to larger circular needle.
Knit 2 rnds.
With B, knit 4 rnds.
Next rnd With A, k3, *k5b, k3; rep from * to last st, k5b.
Knit one rnd.
With C, knit 4 rnds.
Next rnd With A, k1, *k5b, k3; rep from * to last 3 sts, k5b, k2.
Knit 1 rnd.
With D, knit 4 rnds.
Next rnd With A, k3, *k5b, k3; rep from * to last st, k5b.
Knit 1 rnd.
With B, knit 4 rnds.
Next rnd With A, k1, *k5b, k3; rep from * to last 3 sts, k5b, k2.
Knit 1 rnd.
With C, knit 4 rnds.
Next rnd With A, k3, *k5b, k3; rep from * to last st, k5b.
Knit 1 rnd.
With D, knit 4 rnds.
Next rnd With A, k1, *k5b, k3; rep from * to last 3 sts, k5b, k2.
Knit 1 rnd.
Cont in pat as est until piece measures approx 6½"/16.5cm from beg. End with 4 rnds in D.

CROWN SHAPING

Note Change to dpns when sts no longer comfortably fit on circular needle.
Rnd 1 With A, *[k3, k5b] 3 times, k3tog, k5b; rep from * around—98 sts.
Rnd 2 *K11, k3tog; rep from * around—84 sts.
Rnds 3–6 With B, knit.
Rnd 7 With A, k1, k5b, k3, k5b, *k3tog, k5b, [k3, k5b] twice; rep from * to last 6 st, k3tog, k5b, k2—70 sts.
Rnd 8 K5, *k3tog, k7; rep from * to last 5 sts, k3tog, k2—56 sts.
Rnds 9–12 With C, knit.
Rnd 13 With A *k3tog, k5b, k3, k5b; rep from * around—42 sts.
Rnd 14 Remove marker, sl 1st st from RH needle to LH needle, replace marker, *k3tog, k3; rep from * around—28 sts.
Rnds 15–18 With D, knit.
Rnd 19 Remove marker, sl 1st st from RH needle to LH needle, replace marker, with A , *k3tog, k5b; rep from * around—14 sts.
Rnd 20 K2tog around—7 sts.
Break yarn, leaving an 8"/20.5cm tail. Thread through rem sts. Pull tog tightly and secure end. ■

Cabled Boot Toppers

Add some panache—and warmth—to your favorite boots by tucking in a pair of Aran toppers.

DESIGNED BY ANN SZWARC, PK YARN OVER KNIT, CLAWSON, MI

Knitted Measurements
Circumference at top 14"/35.5cm
Height 6½"/16.5cm

Materials
■ 1 3½oz/100g hank (each approx 220yd/201m) of Cascade Yarns *Cascade 220* (wool) in #9401 light grey and medium grey tweed
■ One each sizes 6 and 8 (4 and 5mm) circular needle, 16"/40cm long, *or size to obtain gauge*
■ Stitch marker
■ Cable needle (cn)

Stitch Glossary
6-st LC Sl 3 sts to cn, hold to *front*, k3; k3 from cn.
6-st RC Sl 3 sts to cn, hold to *back*, k3; k3 from cn.

K1, P1 Rib
(over an even number of sts)
Rnd 1 *K1, p1; rep from * around.
Rep rnd 1 for k1, p1 rib.

Boot Topper (make 2)
With smaller needle, cast on 84 sts. Join to work in the rnd, being careful not to twist sts, and place marker for beg of rnd. Work in k1, p1 rib for 1½"/4cm. Change to larger needle and purl 1 rnd.

BEG CHART
Note 28-st rep of chart is worked 3 times for each rnd.
Work rnds 1–8 of chart 3 times, then work rnds 1–6 once more.
Next rnd *P2, k2, p1, k3, p1, k2, p2, k1 tbl; rep from * to end of rnd. Rep last rnd 4 times more. Bind off loosely in pat.

Finishing
Block lightly to measurements. ■

Stitch Key
□ Knit
— Purl
Ⴓ K1 tbl
▨ 6-st LC
▨ 6-st RC

Gauge
26 sts and 26 rnds to 4"/10 cm over cable pat using size 8 (5mm) needles.
Take time to check gauge.

Ribs and Buttons Hat

Oversize ribs and a buttoned flap lend simple style to a slouchy, quick-to-knit hat.

DESIGNED BY CORI SCHRADER, GOT YOUR GOAT YARN STUDIO, ROSEVILLE, CA

Size
Woman's Small/Medium

Knitted Measurements
Brim circumference (buttoned and slightly stretched) 18"/45.5cm
Length 10"/25.5cm

Materials
- 1 3½oz/100g hank (each approx 220yd/201m) of Cascade Yarns *Cascade 220 Heathers* (wool) in #9442 baby rose heather
- One each sizes 8 and 10 (5 and 6mm) circular needle, each 16"/40.5cm long, *or size to obtain gauge*
- One set (5) size 10 (6mm) double-pointed needles (dpns)
- Stitch marker
- Tapestry needle
- Two buttons, ¾"/19mm diameter

Notes
1) Brim is worked back and forth in rows on circular needle.
2) Crown is worked in the round on circular needle.

K4, P4 Rib
(multiple of 8 sts)
Row 1 (RS) *K4, p4; rep from * to end.
Row 2 Rep row 1.
Rep rows 1 and 2 for k4, p4 rib.

Hat
With smaller circular needle, cast on 88 sts. Work 22 rows in k4, p4 rib, working buttonholes on rows 6 and 16 as foll:
Next (buttonhole) row (RS) Work in pat to last 8 sts, k2, yo, k2tog, p4. Work 9 rows even.
Next row (RS) Bind off 8 sts, work in pat to end of row—80 sts. Do not turn. Join to work in the rnd, placing marker for beg of rnd.
Rnd 1 Purl. Change to larger needle.
Rnd 2 Knit.
Rnd 3 *K4, M1; rep from * around—100 sts.
Rnd 4 K50, M1, k50, M1—102 sts.
Rnds 5–16 Knit.

CROWN SHAPING
Note Change to dpns when sts no longer comfortably fit on circular needle.
Rnd 1 *K15, k2tog; rep from * around—96 sts. Work 1 rnd even.
Rnd 3 *K14, k2tog; rep from * around—90 sts. Work 1 rnd even.
Rnd 5 *K13, k2tog; rep from * around—84 sts. Work 1 rnd even.
Rnd 7 *K12, k2tog; rep from * around—78 sts. Work 1 rnd even.
Rnd 9 *K11, k2tog; rep from * around—72 sts. Work 1 rnd even.
Rnd 11 *K10, k2tog; rep from * around—66 sts. Work 1 rnd even.
Rnd 13 *K9, k2tog; rep from * around—60 sts. Work 1 rnd even.
Rnd 15 *K8, k2tog; rep from * around—54 sts. Work 1 rnd even.
Rnd 17 *K7, k2tog; rep from * around—48 sts.
Rnd 18 *K6, k2tog; rep from * around—42 sts.
Rnd 19 *K5, k2tog; rep from * around—36 sts.
Rnd 20 *K4, k2tog; rep from * around—30 sts.
Rnd 21 *K3, k2tog; rep from * around—24 sts.
Rnd 22 *K2, k2tog; rep from * around—18 sts.
Rnd 23 *K1, k2tog; rep from * around—12 sts.
Rnd 24 *K2tog; rep from * around—6 sts. Break yarn, leaving 10"/25cm tail. Thread tail through rem sts. Pull tight and secure.

Finishing
Block lightly. Sew on buttons opposite buttonholes. ■

Gauge
16 sts and 20 rows to 4"/10cm over St st using size 10 (6mm) needles.
Take time to check gauge.

11

Flowered Pull-Through Scarf

A statement flower adds drama to a garter-stitch scarf, knit on large needles to provide drape.

DESIGNED BY CANDACE BROEKER, STITCHES IN TIME, BELLFLOWER, CA

Knitted Measurements
Width 9½"/24cm
Length 40"/101.5cm

Materials
■ 2 3½oz/100g hanks (each approx 220yd/201m) of Cascade Yarns *Cascade 220 Paints* (wool) in #9729 red mix

■ One pair each sizes 8 and 10½ (5 and 6.5mm) needles *or size to obtain gauge*

■ Removable stitch marker

Scarf
With smaller needles, cast on 11 sts. Work in garter st (k every row) for 6"/15cm (lightly stretch work before measuring, as loop will stretch slightly with wear).

FORM LOOP
Fold piece in half with working edge at front, cast-on edge at back. If fold line is a space between ridges, knit 1 row more so fold line falls on a ridge.
Knit 1st st on LH needle tog with 1st cast-on stitch; rep for each st on needle (there will be 1 st more on needle than on cast-on edge; k last 2 sts on needle tog with last cast-on st)—11 sts.
Next row (inc) With smaller needle, [k1, yo, k1] in each st across—33 sts. Change to larger needles and work in garter st until piece measures 31"/78.5cm from loop. Bind off.

2ND SCARF END
With smaller needles, pick up and k 1 st in each st on fold line of loop—11 sts.
Next row (inc) [K1, yo, k1] in each st across—33 sts.
Change to larger needles and cont in garter st for 4½"/11.5cm. Bind off.

Flower
With larger needles, cast on 14 sts, leaving 12"/30.5cm tail.
Next row (inc) [K1, yo, k1] in each st across—42 sts.
Knit 2 rows.
Rep inc row—126 sts. Place marker on this row.
Knit 6 rows. Bind off, leaving 18"/45.5cm tail.

Finishing
Using tail from cast-on, gather cast-on edge, pull tightly to secure.
Using tail from bind-off, gather along side edge of work to second inc row (marked row), then gather across second inc row, pull to tighten. Roll tog and adjust to create ruffled flower shape. Sew flower to pull-through loop of scarf. Block lightly to measurements. ■

Gauges
13 sts and 17 rows to 4"/10cm over St st using size 10½ (6.5mm) needles.
14 sts and 23 rows to 4"/10cm over garter st using size 10½ (6.5mm) needles.
Take time to check gauges.

Fair Isle Stockings

Keep warm and show off your colorwork skills when you wear these cozy knee-highs.

DESIGNED BY TAMMY EIGEMAN THOMPSON, WOOLEN COLLECTIBLES, KALISPELL, MT

Size
Adult Small/Medium

Knitted Measurements
Foot circumference 8"/20cm
Foot length 9"/23cm
Height from ankle 20"/51cm
Circumference at top (unstretched)
11"/28cm

Materials
■ 3 1¾oz/50g hanks (each approx
164yd/150m) of Cascade Yarns *Cascade
220 Sport* (wool) in #4002 jet (A)

■ 2 hanks in #8401 silver grey (B)

■ 1 hank in #9456 sapphire heather (C)

■ Size 3 (3.25mm) circular needle,
12"/30.5cm long, *or size to obtain gauge*

■ One set (5) size 3 (3.25mm)
double-pointed needles (dpns)

■ Stitch markers

■ Stitch holders

K1, P1 Rib
(multiple of 2 sts)
Rnd 1 *K1, p1; rep from * to end of rnd.
Rep rnd 1 for k1, p1 rib.

Note
When working chart 2, the 1st st of every
round (center back st) is worked in color
A. This st is not included in the chart.

Stocking (make 2)
With circular needle and A, cast on 80
sts. Join to work in the rnd, taking care
not to twist sts, and place marker (pm)
for beg of rnd. Work in k1, p1 rib for
5"/13cm.

Next rnd Knit, inc 4 sts evenly around—
84 sts.
Knit 2 rnds in A. Work rnds 1–17 of
chart 1.
Next rnd With A, knit, dec 3 sts evenly
around—81 sts.
Work rnds 1–11 of chart 2, working 1st
st of every rnd in A.

CALF SHAPING
Note Change to dpns when sts no longer
comfortably fit on circular needle.
Work in pat as est, and, AT THE SAME
TIME, dec at center back leg every 3 rnds
as foll:
Next (dec) rnd K1, ssk, work in pat to
last 2 sts, k2tog—2 sts dec.
Cont as est until 65 sts rem. Work even
in pat until piece measures 17"/43cm.

HEEL FLAP
Set-up rnd Work in pat to last 12 sts.
With A only, knit to end, then k11, k2tog
(beg of next rnd). Turn.
Next row P24.
Work chart 3 once over these 24 sts.

TURN HEEL
Row 1 (WS) With A, p12, then p1,
p2tog, p1, turn.

Gauge
28 sts and 30 rows to 4"/10cm over Fair Isle pat using size 3 (3.25mm) needles.
Take time to check gauge.

Fair Isle Stockings

CHART 1

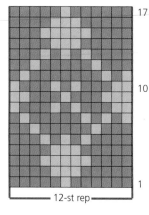

17

10

1

12-st rep

CHART 2

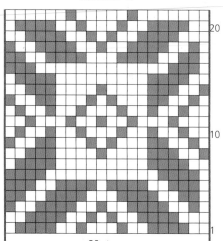

20

10

1

20-st rep

CHART 3

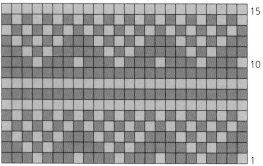

15

10

1

24 sts

CHART 4

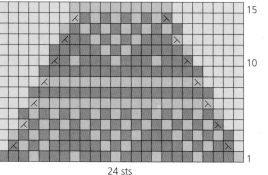

15

10

1

24 sts

Color and Stitch Key

■	Jet (A)
□	Silver grey (B)
▨	Sapphire heather (C)
⊠	Ssk
⊠	K2tog
▨	No stitch

Row 2 Sl 1, k3, ssk, k1, turn.
Row 3 Sl 1, p4, p2tog, p1, turn.
Row 4 Sl 1, k5, ssk, k1, turn.
Cont in pat, working one more st each row until all sts have been worked, ending with RS row.

INSTEP
With dpn, pick up and k 12 sts along heel flap, alternating A and B. Work across top of foot in pat with 2nd dpn. With 3rd dpn, pick up and k 12 sts along heel flap, alternating A and B, and work across 12 heel sts, alternating A and B (new beg of rnd). Rem heel sts will be worked on 1st dpn. Work 1 rnd even.
Next rnd Cont in pat, work across dpn 1 to last 3 sts, k2tog, k1, work across dpn 2, on dpn 3; k1, ssk, work to end—2 sts dec.
Next rnd Work even in pat.
Rep last 2 rnds until 64 sts rem. Work even in pat until foot measures 7½"/19cm or approx 1½"/4cm less than desired length.

TOE SHAPING
With A only, work across dpn 1, dec across dpn 2 as foll: [k1, k2tog twice] 8 times, work across dpn 3. Work across dpn 1 once more (new beg of rnd). Work rnds 1–15 of chart 4.

Finishing
Graft toe sts tog. Block lightly to measurements. ■

Holly Hat

A whimsical appliqué of holly leaves and berries brightens up a fall beanie.

DESIGNED BY PAULA HERBERT, YARN GARDEN, LITTLETON, NH

Size
Woman's Medium

Knitted Measurements
Brim circumference 19"/48cm
Height 7½"/ 19cm

Materials
- 1 3½oz/100g hank (each approx 220yd/201m) of Cascade Yarns *Cascade 220* (wool) each in #8911 grape jelly (A) and #0980 pesto (B)
- Size 9 (5.5mm) circular needle, 16"/40cm long, *or size to obtain gauge*
- One set (5) size 9 (5.5mm) double-pointed needles (dpns)
- One pair size 3 (3.25mm) needles
- Stitch markers
- Tapestry needle

Note
When working top of hat, decreases in St st sections are always k2tog/ssk while decreases in seed st sections need to be either p2tog/p2tog tbl *or* k2tog/ssk as necessary to maintain seed st pattern.

Hat
With circular needle and A, cast on 76 sts. Join to work in the rnd, being careful not to twist sts, and place marker (pm) for beg of rnd.
Knit 6 rows in St st. Join B. (Don't cut A; twist A with B at the beginning of each row to carry up.) Knit 1 rnd, purl 2 rnds, knit 1 rnd. Cut B. Cont with A as foll:

Gauge
16 sts and 22 rows to 4"/10cm over St st using size 9 (5.5mm) needles.
Take time to check gauge.

Holly Hat

Rnd 1 [K19, pm, (k1, p1) 9 times, k1, pm] twice.
Rnd 2 [K19, sl m, (p1, k1) 9 times, p1, sl m] twice.
Rnd 3 [K19, sl m, (k1, p1) 9 times, k1, sl m] twice.
Rep rnds 2 and 3 until piece measures approx 5"/13cm from end of contrast trim, ending with rnd 3.

CROWN SHAPING
Note Change to dpns when sts no longer comfortably fit on circular needle.
Rnd 1 (dec) *K2tog, k to 2 sts before marker, ssk, sl m, p2tog/k2tog as needed to maintain pat, work in seed st to 2 sts before marker, p2tog tbl/ssk as needed to maintain pat; rep from * once more.
Rnd 2 Work even in est pat.
Rep rnds 1 and 2 until 5 sts rem between markers. Work one more dec row. Break yarn, leaving an 6"/15cm tail. Thread through rem sts. Pull tog tightly and secure end.

Leaves and Berries
LEAVES (MAKE 2)
With smaller needles and B, cast on 3 sts.
Row 1 (RS) K1, yo, k1, yo, k1—5 sts.
Row 2 (WS) Purl.
Row 3 K2, yo, k1, yo, k2—7 sts.
Row 4 Purl.

Row 5 K3, yo, k1, yo, k3—9 sts.
Row 6 Purl.
Row 7 Ssk, k5, k2tog—7 sts.
Row 8 P2tog, p3, p2tog tbl—5 sts.
Row 9 K2, yo, k1, yo, k2—7 sts.
Row 10 Purl.
Row 11 K3, yo, k1, yo, k3—9 sts.
Row 12 Purl.
Row 13 Ssk, k5, k2tog—7 sts.
Row 14 P2tog, p3, p2tog tbl—5 sts.
Row 15 Ssk, k1, k2tog—3 sts.
Row 16 P2tog, p1, slip first st over second. Cut 6"/15cm tail and pull through last stitch.

BERRIES (MAKE 3)
With smaller needles and A, cast on 5 sts.
Purl across row. Slip all sts one at a time over the last st worked and slip off needle. Break yarn and thread through rem st. Pull tightly.

Finishing
Block hat and leaves lightly, pinning leaves to shape. Use tails on leaves and berries to attach, using photo as guide. Weave in rem ends. ∎

Cabled Earflap Hat

Keep your ears covered and your style on display with cables, braids, and a fun oversize tassel.

DESIGNED BY CYNTHIA SPENCER, STITCH YOUR ART OUT, PINE GROVE MILLS, PA

Size
Adult Medium

Knitted Measurements
Brim circumference 21"/53.5cm
Length (excluding earflaps) 8"/20cm

Materials
- 1 3½oz/100g hank (each approx 220yd/201m) of Cascade Yarns *Cascade 220* (wool) in #8894 Christmas green
- Size 7 (4.5mm) circular needle, 16"/40.5cm long, *or size to obtain gauge*
- One set (5) size 7 (4.5mm) double-pointed needles (dpns)
- Size 5 (3.75mm) circular needle, 16"/40.5cm long
- Stitch markers
- Stitch holders
- Cable needle (cn)
- Tapestry needle

Stitch Glossary
K1b Insert right needle tip into st one row below next st on left needle and bring onto left needle, knit this st.
4-st LC Sl 2 sts to cn and hold to *front*, k2, k2 from cn.
3-st LPC Sl 2 sts to cn and hold to *front*, p1, k2 from cn.
3-st RPC Sl 1 st to cn and hold to *back*, k2, p1 from cn.

Hat
EAR FLAPS
With smaller needle, cast on 4 sts. Knit one row.
Set-up row [K1, yo] three times, k1—7 sts.
Row 1 (RS) Sl 1, knit to end.
Row 2 Sl 1, k1b, knit to last 2 sts, k1b, k1—2 sts inc.
Rows 3–6 Sl 1, knit to end.
Rep rows 1–6 five times more—19 sts. Place first earflap on holder. Rep for second earflap.

JOINING FLAPS TO HAT
With smaller needle, cast on 9 sts. With RS facing, knit across one earflap, cast on 44 sts, knit across second earflap, cast on 9 sts—100 sts.

Join to work in the rnd, taking care not to twist sts, and place marker (pm) for beg of rnd.
Work in garter st (purl one rnd, knit one rnd) for approx 1"/2.5cm, ending with a purl rnd.
Next rnd Knit, inc 8 sts evenly around using k1b. AT THE SAME TIME, pm every 12 sts—108 sts.
Change to larger circular needle and work rnds 1–23 of chart, rep chart between markers.

CROWN SHAPING
Note Change to dpns when sts no longer comfortably fit on circular needle.
Rnds 1–3 [P4, k4, p4] around.
Rnd 4 [P4, 4-st LC, p4] around.
Rnd 5 *P2, p2tog, k4, pm, p4, remove marker; rep from * to last 4 sts—99 sts. Pm for beg of rnd.
Rnd 6 [P7, k4] around, remove original beg of rnd marker.
Rnd 7 [P7, k4] around.
Rnd 8 [P5, p2tog, 4-st LC] around—90 sts.
Rnd 9 [P6, k4] around.
Rnd 10 [P4, p2tog, k4] around—81 sts.
Rnd 11 [P5, k4] around.
Rnd 12 [P3, p2tog, 4-st LC] around—72 sts.

Gauge
20 sts and 28 rows to 4"/10cm over St st using size 7 (4.5mm) needles.
Take time to check gauge.

Rnd 13 [P4, k4] around.
Rnd 14 [P2, p2tog, k4] around—63 sts.
Rnd 15 [P3, k4] around.
Rnd 16 [P1, p2tog, 4-st LC] around—54 sts.
Rnd 17 [P2, k4] around.
Rnd 18 [P2tog, k4] around—45 sts.
Rnd 19 [P1, k4] around.
Rnd 20 [P1, 4-st LC] around.
Rnd 21 [P1, (k2tog) twice] around—27 sts.
Rnd 22 [P1, k2] around.
Rnd 23 [P1, k2tog] around—18 sts.
Rnd 24 K2tog around—9 sts.
Break yarn, leaving an 8"/20cm tail.
Thread tail through rem sts. Pull tight and secure.

Finishing
BRAIDS
Wind yarn around a book approx 11"/28cm high 36 times. Cut the yarn at one end to make 36 individual strands. Use 3 groups of 6 strands for each earflap. Using a tapestry needle, thread 6 strands through each eyelet hole at bottom of earflap. Pull even and braid the groups of strands. Tie end securely. Trim.

TASSEL
Wrap 9 more strands around book and cut. Braid 6 strands together, knotting at each end. Set aside rem 3 strands. Wrap enough yarn for a thick tassel around a book approx 8"/20cm tall. Thread rem 3 strands under wrapped yarn and knot tightly. Fold tassel in half with knotted yarn at top. Wrap braid around tassel, approx 1"/2.5cm from top, and tie securely. Trim. Sew to top of hat. Block lightly to measurements. ■

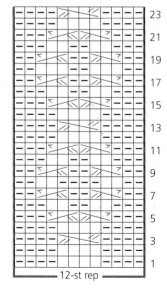

— 12-st rep —

23
21
19
17
15
13
11
9
7
5
3
1

Stitch Key

□ Knit

− Purl

 3-st RPC

3-st LPC

4-st LC

42

Leaf Headband

A simple headband turns into something special for springtime with short-row shaping and leaf ties.

DESIGNED BY KATHRYN MAYNARD, KNITTERS MERCANTILE, COLUMBUS, OH

■■■▫

Knitted Measurements
Width (at widest point) 5"/12.5cm
Length 30"/76cm

Materials
■ 1 3½oz/100g hank (each approx 220yd/201m) of Cascade Yarns *Cascade 220 Heathers* (wool) in #9461 lime heather

■ One pair size 4 (3.5mm) needles *or size to obtain gauge*

■ Stitch markers

■ Size E/4 (3.5mm) crochet hook and waste yarn for provisional cast-on

Provisional Cast-on
Using scrap yarn and crochet hook, ch the number of sts to cast on plus a few extra. Cut a tail and pull the tail through the last chain. With knitting needle and yarn, pick up and knit the stated number of sts through the "purl bumps" on the back of the chain. To remove waste chain, when instructed, pull out the tail from the last crochet stitch. Gently and slowly pull on the tail to unravel the crochet stitches, carefully placing each released knit stitch on a needle.

Short Row Wrap and Turn (W&T)
on RS row (on WS row)
1) Wyib (wyif), sl next st purlwise.
2) Move yarn between the needles to the front (back).
3) Sl the same st back to LH needle. Turn work. One st is wrapped.
4) When working the wrapped st, insert RH needle under the wrap and work it tog with the corresponding st on needle.

Notes
1) The second leaf tip is worked after main section by removing provisional cast-on.
2) Slip sts purlwise with yarn in back.

Headband
Using a provisional cast-on, cast on 5 sts.
Rows 1, 3, and 5 (RS) K5.
Rows 2, 4, and 6 K2, p1, k2.
Row 7 K1, kfb, k1, kfb, k1—7 sts.
Row 8 K3, p1, k3.
Row 9 K1, kfb, k3, kfb, k1—9 sts.
Row 10 K4, p1, k4.
Row 11 K5, m1, k4—10 sts.
Rows 12 and 14 K4, p to last 4 sts, k4.
Row 13 K5, m1, sl 1, k4—11 sts.
Row 15 K5, m1, k to last 5 sts, sl 1, k4—12 sts.

Gauge
22 sts and 32 rows to 4"/10cm over St st using size 4 (3.5mm) needles.
Take time to check gauge.

Row 16 K4, p to last 4 sts, k4.
Rep last 2 rows 18 times more, end with a WS row—30 sts.
Next row (RS) K4, sl 1, k to last 5 sts, sl 1, k4.
Next row K4, p to last 4 sts, k4.
Rep last 2 rows 11 times more, end with a WS row.

BEG SHORT ROW SHAPING
Short row 1 (RS) K4, sl 1, k14, w&t, p to last 4 sts, k4.
Row 2 (RS) K4, sl 1, k to last 5 sts, picking up wrap, sl 1, k4.
Rows 3 and 5 K4, p to last 4 sts, k4.
Row 4 K4, sl 1, k to last 5 sts, sl, k4.
Rep rows 1–4 once more, then row 1 once.
Next row (RS) K4, sl 1, k to last 5 sts, sl 1, k4.
Next row K4, p to last 4 sts, k4.
Rep last 2 rows 11 times more, end with a WS row.
Next row (RS) K4, ssk, k to last 5 sts, sl 1, k4—29 sts.
Next row K4, p to last 4 sts, k4.
Rep last 2 rows 19 times more, end with a WS row—10 sts.

BEG TAPER AND FIRST LEAF TIP
Row 1 (RS) K4, ssk, k4—9 sts.
Row 2 K4, p1, k4.
Row 3 K1, ssk, k3, k2tog, k1—7 sts.
Row 4 K3, p1, k3.
Row 5 K1, ssk, k1, k2tog, k1—5 sts.
Rows 6, 8, 10, and 12 K2, p1, k2.
Rows 7, 9, and 11 K5.
Row 13 K1, kfb, k1, kfb, k1—7 sts.
Row 14 K3, p1, k3.
Row 15 K1, kfb, k3, kfb, k1—9 sts.
Row 16 K4, place marker (pm), p1, pm, k4.

Row 17 K4, sm, yo, k1, yo, sm, k4—11 sts.
Row 18 K to first maker, p to second marker, k to end of row.
Rep last 2 rows 5 times more, end with a WS row—21 sts.
Rows 29, 31, and 33 K21.
Rows 30, 32, and 34 K4, p13, k4.
Row 35 K4, ssk, k to last 6 sts, k2tog, k4—19 sts.
Row 36 K4, p to last 4 sts, k4.
Rep last 2 rows 4 times more, end with a WS row—11 sts.
Row 45 K4, SK2P, k4—9 sts.
Row 46 K4, p1, k4.
Row 47 K1, ssk, k3, k2tog, k1—7 sts.
Row 48 K7.
Row 49 K1, ssk, k1, k2tog, k1—5 sts.
Row 50 K5.
Row 51 K1, SK2P, k1—3 sts.
Row 52 SK2P—1 st. Fasten off.

SECOND LEAF TIP
Undo provisional cast-on and place sts on needle, ready for a RS row—5 sts. Join yarn.
Row 1 (RS) K5.
Row 2 K2, p1, k2.
Rep rows 13–52 of first leaf tip.

Finishing
Block to measurements. ■

Windmill & Flower Mittens

Go Dutch with these charming Fair Isle mittens that feature windmills and tulips.

DESIGNED BY KELLY NORBY, LE MOUTON ROUGE KNITTERY, MORRIS, IL

Size
Woman's Small/Medium

Knitted Measurements
Hand circumference 7½"/19cm
Length 8¾"/22cm

Materials
- 1 1¾oz/50g hank (each approx 273yd/250m) of Cascade Yarns *Cascade 220 Fingering* (wool) each in #9332 sapphire (A), #4147 lemon yellow (B), #9592 sage (C), and #8012 doeskin heather (D)
- One set (5) size 3 (3.25mm) double-pointed needles (dpns) *or size to obtain gauge*
- Stitch markers
- Stitch holders or waste yarn
- Tapestry needle

Stitch Glossary
M1R Make 1 right: Insert LH needle from back to front under the strand between last st worked and next st on LH needle. K into the front loop to twist the st.
M1L Make 1 left: Insert LH needle from front to back under the strand between last st worked and next st on LH needle. K into the back loop to twist the st.

K2, P2 Rib
(multiple of 4 sts)
Rnd 1 K2, p2; rep from * to end of rnd.
Rep rnd 1 for k2, p2 rib.

Mitten (make 2)
With A, cast on 72 sts. Join to work in the rnd, taking care not to twist sts, and place marker (pm) for beg of rnd. Work 6 rnds in k2, p2 rib. Knit 1 rnd.

BEG CHARTS 1 AND 2
Work rnds 1–7 of chart 1 (2 reps of each rnd).
Cont working rnds 8–28, AT THE SAME TIME, work chart 2 for gusset, adding new sts in the spot indicated on chart 1 for left or right mitten.
Rnd 29 Work as est to end of thumb gusset sts. Slip 21 thumb gusset sts just worked onto holder, cont to end of rnd. Work rnds 30–84 of chart. Break yarns. Graft rem sts tog with A.

THUMB
Place 21 sts on holder back on needles, dividing evenly among 3 needles. Beg at inside of gusset, using A, pick up and k 4 sts from hand—25 sts. Work rnds 1–23 of chart 3.
Break yarns. Graft rem sts tog with A.

Finishing
Block lightly to measurements. ■

Gauge
36 sts and 42 rows to 4"/10cm over St st using size 3 (3.25mm) needles.
Take time to check gauge.

Windmill & Flower Mittens

CHART 1

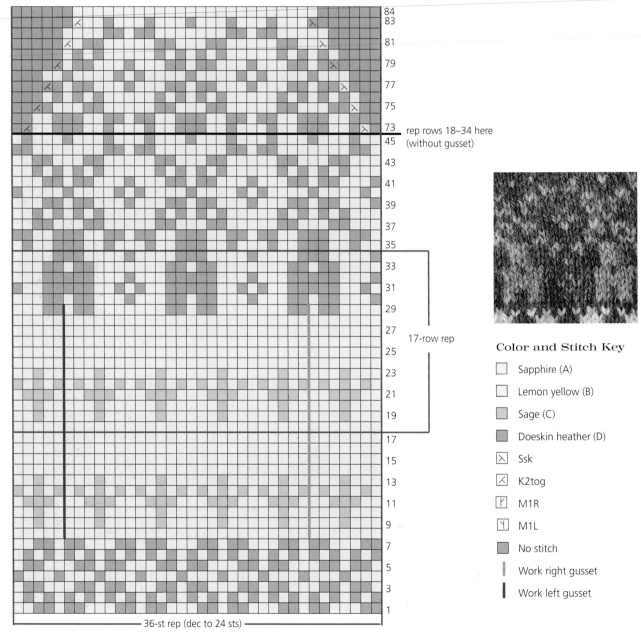

84
83
81
79
77
75
73 — rep rows 18–34 here (without gusset)
45
43
41
39
37
35
33
31
29 } 17-row rep
27
25
23
21
19
17
15
13
11
9
7
5
3
1

36-st rep (dec to 24 sts)

Color and Stitch Key

☐	Sapphire (A)
☐	Lemon yellow (B)
▨	Sage (C)
▨	Doeskin heather (D)
⊠	Ssk
⊠	K2tog
⅄	M1R
⅄	M1L
▨	No stitch
⏐	Work right gusset
▮	Work left gusset

CHART 2

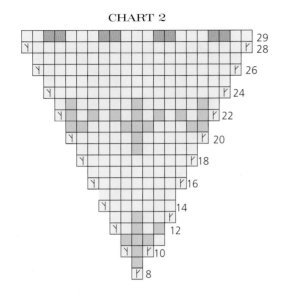

CHART 3

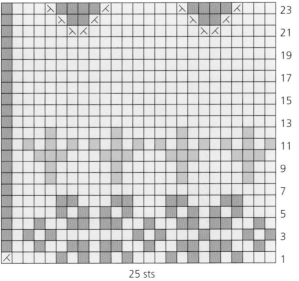

25 sts

Lacy Cables Hat

A clever combination of design elements: bands of lacy cables on a purl background form a uniquely lovely ribbing.

DESIGNED BY ANDREA MAGLISCEAU, THE WOOLIE EWE, PLANO, TX

Size
Woman's Medium

Knitted Measurements
Brim circumference 22"/(56)cm

Materials
■ 2 3½oz/100g hanks (each approx 220yd/201m) of Cascade Yarns *Cascade 220* (wool) in #7812 lagoon

■ One each sizes 5 and 7 (3.75 and 4.5mm) circular needle, 16"/41cm long, *or size to obtain gauge*

■ One set (5) size 5 (3.75mm) double-pointed needles (dpns)

■ Stitch marker

Stitch Glossary
Pfb Purl into front and back of next st— 1 st increased.

Hat
With dpns, cast on 6 sts and distribute among 3 needles. (Add a 4th dpn as number of sts increases.)
Join to work in the rnd, being careful not to twist sts, and place marker (pm) for beg of rnd.
Rnd 1 Knit.
Rnd 2 [K1, yo] 6 times—12 sts.
Rnd 3 Knit.
Rnd 4 [Yo, k1] 12 times—24 sts.
Rnd 5 Knit.
Rnd 6 [K2, yo] 12 times—36 sts.
Rnd 7 Knit.
Rnd 8 [Yo, k3] 12 times—48 sts.
Rnd 9 Knit.
Rnd 10 [K1, yo, k2tog, yo, k1] 12 times— 60 sts.
Rnd 11 Knit.
Rnd 12 [Yo, ssk, k2tog, yo, kfb] 12 times—72 sts.
Rnd 13 [K5, p1] 12 times.
Rnd 14 [K1, yo, sl 1, k2tog, psso, yo, k1, pfb] 12 times—84 sts.

Change to smaller circular needle, pm for beg of rnd.
Rnd 15 [K5, p2] 12 times.
Rnd 16 [Yo, ssk, k1, k2tog, yo, pfb, p1] 12 times—96 sts.
Rnd 17 [K5, p3] 12 times.
Rnd 18 [K1, yo, sl 1, k2tog, psso, yo, k1, p3] 12 times.
Rnd 19 [K5, p3] 12 times.
Rnd 20 [Yo, ssk, k1, k2tog, yo, p3] 12 times.
Rnd 21 [K5, p3] 12 times.
Rep rnds 18–21 until hat measures 7"/18cm.

BEG RIBBING
Switch to smaller circular needle.
Rnd 1 *P2, k1, p2, k3; rep from * to end of rnd.
Rep rnd 1 for 3"/7.5cm. Bind off as foll: P1, *place st back on LH needle, p2tog; rep from * to end.

Finishing
Block lightly to measurements. ■

Gauges
18 sts and 24 rows to 4"/10cm over St st using size 7 (4.5mm) needles.
20 sts and 24 rows to 4"/10cm over lace pat using size 7 (4.5mm) needles.
Take time to check gauges.

Sporty Striped Hat

Stripe a bright color with a neutral gray and you get a sweet and versatile cap for a little cutie.

DESIGNED BY CLAUDIA BARBO, APPLE YARNS, BELLINGHAM, WA

Size
Toddler

Knitted Measurements
Brim circumference 16"/40.5cm
Height 6½"/16.5cm

Materials
■ 1 3½oz/100g ball (each approx 220yd/201m) of Cascade Yarns *220 Superwash* (superwash wool) in #900 charcoal (MC)

■ 1 hank in #851 lime OR #849 dark aqua OR #1952 blaze (CC)

■ One each sizes 5 and 6 (3.75 and 4.25mm) circular needle, each 16"/40.5cm long, *or size to obtain gauge*

■ One set (5) size 5 (3.75mm) double-pointed needles (dpns)

■ Tapestry needle

■ Stitch markers

Hat
With smaller needles and MC, cast on 72 sts. Join to work in the rnd, being careful not to twist sts, and place marker for beg of rnd. Work 6 rnds garter st

(k 1 rnd, p 1 rnd). Change to larger needles, knit 2 rnds.
Work inc rnds as foll:
Rnd 1 *K9, M1; rep from * to end—80 sts.
Rnd 2 *K10, M1; rep from * to end—88 sts.
Rnd 3 *K11, m1; rep from * to end—96 sts.
Cont in St st, alternating MC and CC every 2 rnds beg with MC, for 14 rnds. Drop MC and cont in CC until hat measures 4"/10cm from beg.

CROWN SHAPING
Note Change to dpns when sts no longer comfortably fit on circular needle.
Rnd 1 *K10, k2tog; rep from * to end—88 sts.
Rnd 2 and all even-numbered rnds Knit.
Rnd 3 *K9, k2tog; rep from * to end—80 sts.
Rnd 5 *K8, k2tog; rep from * to end—72 sts.
Rnd 7 *K7, k2tog; rep from * to end—64 sts.
Rnd 9 *K6, k2tog; rep from * to end—56 sts.
Rnd 11 *K5, k2tog; rep from * to end—48 sts.
Rnd 13 *K4, k2tog; rep from * to end—40 sts.
Rnd 15 *K3, k2tog; rep from * to end—32 sts.
Rnd 17 *K2, k2tog; rep from * to end—24 sts.
Rnd 19 *K1, k2tog; rep from * to end—16 sts.
Rnd 21 *K2tog; rep from * to end—8 sts.
Break yarn, leaving a long tail. Thread yarn through remaining sts and pull to secure.

Finishing
Block lightly to measurements. ■

Gauge
22 sts and 32 rows to 4"/10cm over St st using size 6 (4.25mm) needles. *Take time to check gauge.*

Animal Vests

Take your pick of three different cute critters to embellish these colorful baby vests.

DESIGNED BY MARCIE BROOKS, FIBERWORKS, BEAVERCREEK, OH

Sizes
Instructions are written for 6 months. Changes for 12, 18, and 24 months are in parentheses.

Knitted Measurements
Chest circumference 19 (20, 21, 22)"/ 48 (51, 53.5, 56)cm
Length 9½ (10½, 11½, 12)"/ 24 (26.5, 29, 30.5)cm

Materials
FOR DUCK
■ 1 3½oz/100g ball (each approx 220yd/201m) of Cascade Yarns *220 Superwash Quatros* (superwash wool) in #1931 summerdaze (MC)
FOR BEAR
■ 1 3½oz/100g ball (each approx 220yd/201m) of Cascade Yarns *220 Superwash Quatros* (superwash wool) in #1930 green tea (MC)

FOR SQUIRREL
■ 1 3½oz/100g ball (each approx 220yd/201m) hank of Cascade Yarns *220 Superwash Quatros* (superwash wool) in #1932 butterscotch (MC)
FOR ALL
■ 1 3½oz/100g ball (each approx 220yd/201m) of Cascade Yarns *220 Superwash* (superwash wool) in #890 emerald city (CC)
■ One pair size 7 (4.5mm) needles *or size to obtain gauge*
■ Four buttons, ⅝"/15mm diameter

Seed Stitch
(over an even number of sts)
Row 1 (RS) *K1, p1; rep from * to end of row.
Row 2 K the purl and p the knit sts.
Rep row 2 for seed st.

Notes
1) Vest is worked in one piece to armhole.
2) Basic instructions for vest are given, using desired MC.
3) Chart placement for each animal is given on row 7. Follow the row 7 given for desired animal.

Vest
With size 7 (4.5mm) needles and MC, cast on 96 (100, 104, 108) sts. Work 2 rows in seed st.
Row 3 (buttonhole) (RS) K1, k2tog, yo, work in seed st to end of row.
Row 4 Work in seed st to end of row.
Row 5 (RS) Work 4 sts in seed st, knit to last 4 sts, work last 4 sts in seed st.
Row 6 Work 4 sts in seed st, knit to last 4 sts, work last 4 sts in seed st.

CHART SET-UP (DUCK)
Row 7 (RS) With MC, work 4 sts in seed st, k 2 (4, 0, 2), work 12-st rep of chart 1 a total of 7 (7, 8, 8) times, with MC, k 2 (4, 0, 2), work last 4 sts in seed st.

CHART SET-UP (BEAR)
Row 7 (RS) With MC, work 4 sts in seed st, k 2 (4, 0, 1), work 14-st rep of chart 2 a total of 6 (6, 6, 7) times, work sts 1–13 of chart 2 another 0 (0, 0, 1) time, with MC, k 2 (4, 0, 1), work last 4 sts in seed st.

CHART SET-UP (SQUIRREL)
Row 7 (RS) With MC, work 4 sts in seed st, k 0 (2, 4, 1), work 11-st rep of chart 3 a total of 8 (8, 8, 9) times, with MC, k 0 (2, 4, 1), work last 4 sts in seed st.

Gauge
18 sts and 25 rows to 4"/10cm over St st using size 7 (4.5mm) needles.
Take time to check gauge.

Animal Vests

Cont as now est, keeping first and last 4 sts in seed st and working appropriate row to end of desired chart, then cont with MC only, working buttonhole at beg of rows 9 (9, 11, 11), 15 (15, 19, 19) and 21 (21, 27, 27).

Work even in pat until piece measures 4 (4, 4½, 4½)"/10 (10, 11.5, 11.5)cm from beg, end with a WS row.

NECK SHAPING

Next (dec) row (RS) Work 4 sts in seed st, skp, knit to last 6 sts, k2tog, work last 4 sts in seed st—94 (98, 102, 106) sts. Work 3 rows even.

Next (dec) row (RS) Work 4 sts in seed st, skp, knit to last 6 sts, k2tog, work last 4 sts in seed st—92 (96, 100, 104) sts. Work 1 row even.

DIVIDE FOR FRONT/BACK

Next row Work 4 sts in seed st, k 16 (17, 18, 19), work next 4 sts in seed st, turn and leave rem sts on holder—24 (25, 26, 27) sts.

RIGHT FRONT

Keeping first and last 4 sts in seed st, dec 1 st at neck edge every 4th row from previous dec 7 (8, 9, 10) times more—17 sts. Work even in pat until piece measures 9½ (10½, 11½, 12)"/24 (26.5, 29, 30.5)cm from beg, end with a WS row. Bind off rem 17 sts for shoulder.

Back

Place next 44 (46, 48, 50) sts from holder on needle, ready for a RS row.

Row 1 (RS) Work 4 sts in seed st, k 36 (38, 40, 42), work last 4 sts in seed st. Keeping first and last 4 sts in seed st, work even in pat until piece measures 9½ (10½, 11½, 12)"/24 (26.5, 29, 30.5)cm from beg, end with a WS row.

Bind off all sts.

Left front

Place last 24 (25, 26, 27) sts from holder on needle, ready for a RS row.

Row 1 (RS) Work 4 sts in seed st, k19, work last 4 sts in seed st.

Keeping first and last 4 sts in seed st, dec 1 st at neck edge every 4th row from previous dec 7 (8, 9, 10) times more—17 sts. Work even in pat until piece measures 9½ (10½, 11½, 12)"/24 (26.5, 29, 30.5)cm from beg, end with a WS row. Bind off rem 17 sts for shoulder.

Finishing

Block lightly to measurements. Sew shoulder seams. Sew buttons to left front opposite buttonholes. ∎

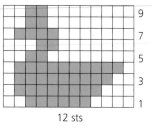

CHART 1

9
7
5
3
1

12 sts

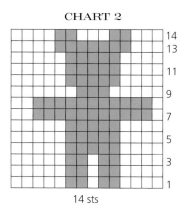

CHART 2

14
13
11
9
7
5
3
1

14 sts

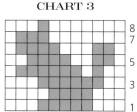

CHART 3

8
7
5
3
1

11 sts

Color Key

☐ Summerdaze, green tea, or butterscotch (MC)

▨ Emerald city (CC)

Two-Way Cabled Beanie

Cables on the crown are picked up from a cabled brim—
or knit just the brim for a cozy headband!

DESIGNED BY MARYSUE FRENCH, CABLED FIBER STUDIO, PORT ANGELES, WA

Size
Woman's Medium

Knitted Measurements
Brim circumference 17"/43cm

Materials
■ 1 3½oz/100g hank (each approx 220yd/201m) of Cascade Yarns *Cascade 220 Heathers* (wool) in #9451 Lake Chelan heather
■ Size 7 (4.5mm) circular needle, 16"/41cm long, *or size to obtain gauge*
■ One set (5) size 7 (4.5mm) double-pointed needles (dpns)
■ Stitch markers
■ Cable needle (cn)
■ Scrap yarn and crochet hook for provisional cast-on

Stitch Glossary
LT Knit tbl of 2nd st on LH needle, do not drop from needle, knit 1st st, then drop sts from needle.
RT Knit 2nd st on LH needle, do not drop from needle, knit 1st st, then drop sts from needle.
6-st LC Sl 3 sts to cn and hold to *front*, k3, k3 from cn.
4-st LC Sl 2 sts to cn and hold to *front*, k2, k2 from cn.

Provisional Cast-On
Using scrap yarn and crochet hook, ch the number of sts to cast on plus a few extra. Cut a tail and pull the tail through the last chain. With knitting needle and yarn, pick up and knit the stated number of sts through the "purl bumps" on the back of the chain. To remove waste chain, when instructed, pull out the tail from the last crochet stitch. Gently and slowly pull on the tail to unravel the crochet stitches, carefully placing each released knit stitch on a needle.

Notes
1) Headband is knitted flat and then grafted together, then sts for hat are picked up from edge.
2) Headband cable is 6 sts wide and 8 rows high; edges are worked in garter st.
3) After 1st row, slip the 1st st of every row purlwise.
4) Change to dpns when sts no longer comfortably fit on circular needle.

Headband
With scrap yarn, cast on 22 sts using provisional cast-on.

Gauges
20 sts and 24 rows to 4"/10cm over St st using size 7 (4.5mm) needles.
24 sts and 26 rows to 4"/10cm over cable pat using size 7 (4.5mm) needles.
Take time to check gauges.

Two-Way Cabled Beanie

Row 1 (RS) K3, p1, LT, p2, k6, p2, RT, p1, k3.
Row 2 and all even-numbered rows
Sl 1, k3, p2, k2, p6, k2, p2, k4.
Rows 3 and 5 Sl 1, k2, p1, LT, p2, k6, p2, RT, p1, k3.
Row 7 Sl 1, k2, p1, LT, p2, 6-st LC, p2, RT, p1, k3.
Rows 9, 11, and 13 Rep row 3.
Row 15 Rep row 7.
Rep rows 8–15 twelve times more.
Rep rows 2 and 3 once more.
Remove scrap yarn from cast-on and place sts onto a dpn.
Graft beg and end of headband tog.

Hat (Optional)
With circular needle, pick up 112 sts evenly to end of rnd edge of headband, join to work in the rnd, place marker (pm) for beg of rnd.
Rnd 1 *K1, p3, k6, p3, k1, pm; rep from * to end of rnd.
Rnds 2–7 *K1, p3, k6, p3, k1, sl marker; rep from * to end of rnd.
Rnd 8 *K1, p3, 6-st LC, p3, k1, sl marker; rep from * to end of rnd.
Rnds 9–14 *K1, p3, k6, p3, k1, sl marker; rep from * to end of rnd.
Rnd 15 *K1, p3, 6-st LC, p3, k1, sl marker; rep from * to end of rnd.
Rnd 16 *K1, p3, k6, p3, k1, sl marker; rep from * to end of rnd.
Rnd 17 (dec) *K1, p1, p2tog, k6, p2tog, p1, k1, sl marker; rep from * to end of rnd—96 sts.
Rnds 18 and 19 *K1, p2, k6, p2, k1; rep from * to end of rnd.
Rnd 20 (dec) *K1, p2tog, k6, p2tog, k1, sl marker; rep from * to end of rnd—80 sts.

Rnds 21 and 22 *K1, p1, k6, p1, k1; rep from * to end of rnd.
Rnd 23 *K1, p1, 6-st LC, p1, k1, remove marker; rep from * to end of rnd, do not remove beg-of-round marker.
Rnd 24 *K1, p1, k6, p1, k1; rep from * to end of rnd.
Rnd 25 K1, *p1, k6, p1, ssk; rep from * to end of rnd, moving marker on last ssk.
Rnd 26 *P1, k6, p1, k1; rep from * to end of rnd.
Rnd 27 *P1, k2, k2tog, k2, p1, k1; rep from * to end of rnd.
Rnd 28 *P1, k5, p1, k1, p1, k2, k2tog, k1, p1, k1; rep from * to end of rnd.
Rnd 29 *P1, k2, k2tog, k1, p1, k1, p1, k4, p1, k1; rep from * to end of rnd.
Rnd 30 *P1, 4-st LC, p2tog; rep from * to end of rnd.
Rnd 31 *P1, k1, k2tog, k1, p1; rep from * to end of rnd.
Rnd 32 P1, *k3, p2tog; rep from * to end of rnd.
Rnd 33 * K1, k2tog, p1; rep from * to end of rnd.
Rnd 34 *K1, k2tog; rep from * to end of rnd.
Rnd 35 * K1, k2tog; rep from * to end of rnd.
Rnd 36 [K1, k2tog] 4 times more, k2tog. Break yarn, leaving an 8"/20.5cm tail. Thread through rem sts. Pull tog tightly and secure end.

Finishing
Block lightly to measurements. ■

Lace-Edged Shawl

This elegant design combines stockinette with a contrast lace edging
and a pretty cable-and-eyelet border at the top.

DESIGNED BY CHRISTINA WILKINS, THE KNITTING NEST, AUSTIN, TX

■■■▭

Knitted Measurements
Width at top Approx 72"/283cm
Height at center Approx 24"/61cm

Materials
■ 2 3½oz/100g hanks (each approx
220yd/201m) of Cascade Yarns *Cascade
220* (wool) each in #7830 coral (A) and
#2413 red (B)
■ One pair size 8 (5mm) needles *or size
to obtain gauge*
■ Cable needle (cn)
■ Stitch markers

Stitch Glossary
4-st LC Sl 2 sts to cn and hold to *front*,
k2, k2 from cn.

Elastic Bind-Off
Purl 2 sts, insert LH needle through
back loops of sts on RH needle, p2tog,
*p1, insert LH needle through back loops
of sts on RH needle, p2tog; rep from *
until desired number of sts have been
bound off.

Lace Pattern
Row 1 (RS) K3, yo, k2tog, k2, [yo, k2tog]
8 times, yo, k2.
Row 2 P23, yo, p2tog, p1.
Row 3 K3, yo, k2tog, k5, [yo, k2tog] 7
times, yo, k2.
Row 4 P24, yo, p2tog, p1.
Row 5 K3, yo, k2tog, k8, [yo, k2tog] 6
times, yo, k2.
Row 6 P25, yo, p2tog, p1.
Row 7 K3, yo, k2tog, k11, [yo, k2tog] 5
times, yo, k2.
Row 8 P26, yo, p2tog, p1.
Row 9 K3, yo, k2tog, k24.
Row 10 Bind off 4 sts, p22, yo,
p2tog, p1.
Rep rows 1–10 for lace pat.

Notes
1) Shawl is knit from side to side. The
contrast edging is worked at same time
as body of shawl.
2) Twist yarns when changing colors to
avoid holes in work.

Gauge
16 sts and 22 rows to 4"/10cm over St st using size 8 (5mm) needles.
Take time to check gauge.

Lace-Edged Shawl

Shawl

With B, cast on 25 sts. Purl one row. Turn work. With A, cast on 3 sts using cable cast-on.

Row 1 (RS) With A, p3, place marker (pm); with B, work row 1 of lace pat. Cont working with A and B as est.

Row 2 Work in lace pat to last 3 sts, k3.

Row 3 P3, M1, sl marker, work in lace pat to end—1 st inc.

Row 4 Work in lace pat to marker, sl marker, p1, k3.

Row 5 P3, k1, M1, sl marker, work in lace pat to end.

Row 6 Work in lace pat to marker, sl marker, p2, k3.

Row 7 P3, k2, M1, sl marker, work in lace pat to end.

Row 8 Work in lace pat to marker, sl marker, p3, k3.

Row 9 P3, k3, M1, sl marker, work in lace pat to end.

Row 10 Work in lace pat to marker, sl marker, p4, k3.

Row 11 P3, k4, M1, sl marker, work in lace pat to end.

Row 12 Work in lace pat to marker, sl marker, k1, p4, k3.

Row 13 P3, k4, p1, M1, sl marker, work in lace pat to end.

Row 14 Work in lace pat to marker, sl marker, p1, k1, p4, k3.

Row 15 P3, 4-st LC, p1, k1, M1, sl marker, twist yarn, work in lace pat to end.

Row 16 Work in lace pat to marker, sl marker, p2, k1, p4, k3.

Row 17 P3, k4, p1, yo, k2tog, M1, sl marker, work in lace pat to end.

Row 18 Work in lace pat to marker, sl marker, p3, k1, p4, k3.

Row 19 P3, 4-st LC, p1, yo, k2tog, k1, pm, M1, sl marker, work in lace pat to end.

Row 20 Work in lace pat to marker, sl marker, p1, sl marker, p3, k1, p4, k3—37 sts: 12 sts in A; 25 sts in B.

Cont in pat, AT THE SAME TIME, work inc row as foll: Inc every RS row 3 times, work 3 rows even, inc on next RS row, work 3 rows even (4 inc rows total).

Inc row (RS) Work 11 sts in pat as est, k to marker, M1 with A, sl marker, work in lace pat to end.

Cont with inc pat until 97 sts rem (72 sts in A; 25 sts in B).

Cont in pat, AT THE SAME TIME, work dec row as foll: Dec every RS row 3 times, work 3 rows even, dec on next RS row, work 3 rows even (total of 4 dec rows).

Dec row (RS) Work in pat to 2 sts before marker, k2tog, sl marker, work in pat to end.

Work dec pat until 37 sts rem (12 sts in A; 25 sts in B). Work final rows as foll:

Row 1 (RS) P3, k4, p1, k1, k2tog, sl marker, work in lace pat to end—1 st dec.

Row 2 Work in lace pat to marker, sl marker, p2, k1, p4, k3.

Row 3 P3, 4-st LC, p1, k2tog, sl marker, work in lace pat to end.

Row 4 Work in lace pat to marker, sl marker, p1, k1, p4, k3.

Row 5 P3, k4, k2tog, sl marker, work in lace pat to end.

Row 6 Work in lace pat to marker, sl marker, p5, k3.

Row 7 P3, k3, k2tog, sl marker, work in lace pat to end.

Row 8 Work in lace pat to marker, sl marker, p4, k3.

Row 9 P3, k2, k2tog, sl marker, work in lace pat to end.

Row 10 Work in lace pat to marker, sl marker, p3, k3.

Row 11 P3, k1, k2tog, sl marker, work in lace pat to end.

Row 12 Work in lace pat to marker, sl marker, p2, k3.

Row 13 P3, k2tog, sl marker, work in lace pat to end.

Row 14 Work in lace pat to marker, sl marker, p1, k3

Row 15 P2, p2tog, sl marker, work in lace pat to end.

Row 16 Work in lace pat to marker, sl marker, k3.

Row 17 P1, p2tog, sl marker, work in lace pat to end.

Row 18 Work in lace pat to marker, sl marker, k2.

Row 19 P2tog, sl marker, work in lace pat to end.

Bind off purlwise using elastic bind-off.

Finishing

Block lightly to measurements. ∎

Faux-Woven Scarf

Single-row stripes worked lengthwise in seed stitch create a classic woven look for a great unisex gift.

DESIGNED BY NANCY VAN HOF, THE SPINNING ROOM, ALTAMONT, NY

■■□□

Knitted Measurements
Length (excluding fringe) 56"/142cm
Width 7¾"/20cm

Materials
■ 1 3½oz/100g hank (each approx 220yd/201m) of Cascade Yarns *Cascade 220* (wool) each in #4002 jet (A), #8400 charcoal (B), #8401 silver grey (C), and #8011 aspen heather (D)

■ Size 5 (3.75mm) circular needle, 24"/cm long, *or size to obtain gauge*

■ Removable stitch markers

■ Tapestry needle

Notes
1) At various points, the color needed will be at the wrong end of the row. Slide the sts to the other end of the needle and work in the opposite direction, continuing in seed stitch as established.
2) Unused yarns are carried up the side of the work until needed. Do not break yarn at the end of the row.

Seed Stitch
(over an odd number of sts)
Row 1 *K1, p1; rep from * to last st, k1.
Rep row 1 for seed st.

Scarf
Cast on 233 sts. Place marker at beg of row 1 to mark RS of work.
Work 8 rows in seed st, switching colors every row as foll: A; B; C; D; B; A; D; C. Cont in est seed st pattern (always knitting the purls and purling the knits), sliding sts to right end of needle and reworking same side when necessary. Change colors as foll:
Row 9 (WS) Color B.
Row 10 (WS) Color D.
Row 11 (RS) Color A.
Row 12 (RS) Color C.
Row 13 (RS) Color D.
Row 14 (RS) Color B.
Row 15 (WS) Color C.
Row 16 (WS) Color A.
Row 17 (WS) Color D.
Row 18 (RS) Color C.
Row 19 (WS) Color B.
Row 20 (RS) Color A.

Row 21 (WS) Color C.
Row 22 (RS) Color D.
Row 23 (WS) Color A.
Row 24 (RS) Color B.
Row 25 (RS) Color C.
Row 26 (RS) Color A.
Row 27 (WS) Color D.
Row 28 (WS) Color B.
Row 29 (WS) Color A.
Row 30 (WS) Color C.
Row 31 (RS) Color B.
Row 32 (RS) Color D.
Row 33 (RS) Color A.
Rep rows 2–32 once more. Slide sts to other end of needle. With A, k5, bind off all sts knitwise to last 5 sts. These final sts will not be bound off. Cut yarn and pull through st on RH needle to fasten off.

Finishing
FRINGE
Unravel 5 sts at each end of the scarf and cut the loops to create the fringe. Trim if necessary.
Lightly block scarf to measurements. ■

Gauge
16 sts and 34 rows to 4"/10cm over St st using size 5 (3.75mm) needles.
Take time to check gauge.

23

Wave Lace Gauntlets

Make a statement for day or night with a pair of lusciously long lacy arm warmers.

DESIGNED BY NANCY TOTTEN, TABLE ROCK LLAMAS FIBER ART STUDIO, BLACK FOREST, CO

■■■□

Size
Woman's Small/Medium

Knitted Measurements
Hand circumference 7"/18cm
Length 11½"/29cm

Materials
■ 2 1¾oz/50g hanks (each approx 136yd/125m) of Cascade Yarns *220 Superwash Sport* (superwash merino) in #827 coral

■ One set (5) size 5 (3.75mm) double-pointed needles (dpns) *or size to obtain gauge*

■ Stitch markers and stitch holder

Stitch Glossary
M1R Insert LH needle from back to front under the strand between last st worked and next st on LH needle. K into the front loop to twist the st.
M1L Insert LH needle from front to back under the strand between last st worked and next st on LH needle. K into the back loop to twist the st.

Gauntlets (make 2)
Cast on 61 sts and join to work in the rnd, being careful not to twist sts. Place marker (pm) for beg of rnd.

EDGING (BOTH HANDS)
Rnd 1 Purl.
Rnd 2 Knit.
Rep rnds 1 and 2 once more.
Next rnd (right hand only) Work 34 sts of chart 1, k27.
Next rnd (left hand only) K27, work 34 sts of chart 1.
Rep this rnd 9 times more.
Cont as est, work charts 2 and 3.
Next rnd (right hand only) Work 30 sts of chart 4, [k1, p1] 3 times, *sl 1 knitwise, p1, psso, place st back on LH needle and pass 2nd st over 1st, move purled st back to RH needle*, [k1, p1] 3 times, rep from * to *, cont [k1, p1] to end of rnd.
Next rnd (left hand only) [K1, p1] 3 times, *sl 1 knitwise, p1, psso, place st back on LH needle and pass 2nd st over 1st, move purled st back to RH needle*, [k1, p1] 3 times, rep from * to *, [k1, p1] for 22 sts, k1, work 30 sts of chart 4. Cont as est through charts 4, 5, and 6, working chart 6 twice ([k1, p1] across all palm sts).

BEG THUMB GUSSET
Next rnd (right hand only) Work rnd 1 of chart 6 for 28 sts, pm, M1R, k1, M1L, pm, work palm sts in [k1, p1].
Next rnd (left hand only) [K1, p1] across palm sts until 1 st rem, pm, M1R, k1, M1L, pm, work rnd 1 of chart 6 for 28 sts. Cont working chart 6 and palm sts as est, AT THE SAME TIME, cont working thumb gusset as foll:
Next rnd Knit.

Gauges
22 sts and 28 rows to 4"/10cm over St st using size 5 (3.75mm) needles.
30 sts and 28 rows to 4"/10cm over pat st using size 5 (3.75mm) needles.
Take time to check gauges.

Wave Lace Gauntlets

CHART 1

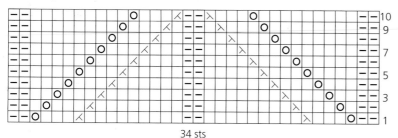

34 sts

CHART 2

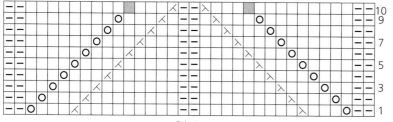

34 sts

CHART 3

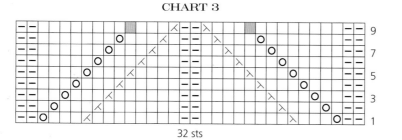

32 sts

Stitch Key

☐	Knit
−	Purl
O	Yo
⟍	Ssk
⟋	K2tog
⟋	P2tog
▨	No stitch

Next rnd (inc) Knit to marker, sl marker, M1R, work to marker, M1L, sl marker, knit to end of rnd.
Cont as est, rep inc rnd every 3rd rnd until there are 15 sts between markers.
Next rnd Work as est to gusset sts, place gusset sts on holder or scrap yarn, cast on 1 st to cover gap, rejoin to work in the rnd.
Cont working until chart 6 has been worked a total of 5 times.

EDGING (BOTH HANDS)
Rnd 1 Knit.
Rnd 2 Purl.
Rep rnds 1 and 2 once more.
Bind off all sts.

THUMB
Place gusset sts from holder onto needles, cast on 1 st, join to work in the rnd. Pm for beg of rnd. Knit 5 rnds. Purl 1 rnd. Bind off.

Finishing
Block lightly to measurements. ■

CHART 4

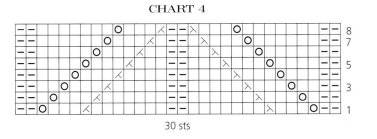

30 sts

CHART 5

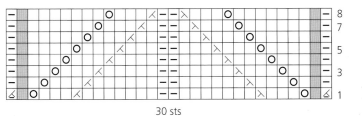

30 sts

CHART 6

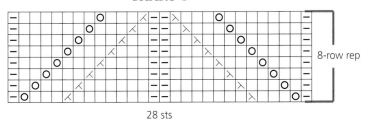

8-row rep

28 sts

Simple Socks

Basic socks don't have to be boring! Use a variegated yarn to make them memorable.

DESIGNED BY BECKY CURRAN, REDLANDS YARN COMPANY, REDLANDS, CA

■■□□

Size
Woman's Medium

Knitted Measurements
Foot circumference 8¼"/21cm
Foot length 9"/23cm
Height from ankle 7"/18cm

Materials
- 1 3½oz/100g balls (each approx 220yd/201m) of Cascade Yarns *220 Superwash Quatros* (superwash wool) in #1954 Malta
- One set (5) size 6 (4mm) double-pointed needles (dpns) *or size to obtain gauge*
- Removable stitch marker
- Tapestry needle

K1, P1 Rib
(multiple of 2 sts)
Rnd 1 *K1, p1; rep from * to end of rnd.
Rep rnd 1 for k1, p1 rib.

Socks (make 2)
Loosely cast on 44 sts and divide among 3 dpns as foll: 12 sts on N1, 20 sts on N2, 12 sts on N3. Join to work in the rnd, being careful not to twist sts, and place marker (pm) for beg of rnd.
Work in k1, p1 rib for 7"/18cm, or until leg of sock is desired length. Move last st of N1 to N2, and move 1st st of N3 to N2 (11 sts on N1, 22 sts on N2, 11 sts on N3).

SET UP FOR HEEL
Set-up row K11 from N1 to N3, p22, turn.
Row 1 (RS) *Sl 1, k1; rep from * to end.
Row 2 (WS) Sl 1, p to end.
Work rows 1 and 2 a total of 11 times.

TURN HEEL
Row 1 (RS) K11, ssk, k1, turn—21 sts.
Row 2 (WS) Sl 1, p1, p2tog, p1, turn—20 sts.
Row 3 Sl 1, k2, ssk, k1, turn—19 sts.
Row 4 Sl 1, p3, p2tog, p1, turn—18 sts.
Row 5 Sl 1, k4, ssk, k1, turn—17 sts.
Row 6 Sl 1, p5, p2tog, p1, turn—16 sts.
Row 7 Sl 1, k6, ssk, k1, turn—15 sts.
Row 8 Sl 1, p7, p2tog, p1, turn—14 sts.
Row 9 Sl 1, k8, ssk, k1, turn—13 sts.
Row 10 Sl 1, p9, p2tog, p1, turn—12 sts.

BEG GUSSET
Knit 12 heel sts (N1). With same needle and RS facing, pick up and k 13 sts down side of heel flap, including 1 st in gusset corner—25 sts on N1. Using an empty needle, knit 22 sts on N2. Using another empty needle, pick up and k 13 sts up 2nd side of heel flap, including 1 st in gusset corner. This is now N3. Knit 1st 6 sts from N1 onto N3 (19 sts on N1, 22 sts on N2, 19 sts on N3).
Rnds 1–3 N1: Knit to last 3 sts, k2tog, k1. N2: Knit. N3: K1, ssk, knit to end.
Rnd 4 Knit.
Rnd 5 N1: Knit to last 3 sts, k2tog, k1. N2: Knit. N3: K1, ssk, knit to end.
Rnds 6–13 Rep rnds 4 and 5 four times more—44 sts (11 sts on N1, 22 sts on N2, 11 sts on N3).

FOOT
Cont in St st until sock (from back of heel to sts on needles) measures 7"/18cm.
Rnd 1 (dec) N1: K to last 3 sts, k2tog, k1. N2: K1, ssk, k to last 3 sts, k2tog, k1. N3: K1, ssk, k to end.
Rnd 2 Knit.
Rep rnds 1 and 2 until 4 sts rem on N1, 8 sts rem on N2, and 4 sts rem on N3. K4 from N1 onto N3.

Finishing
Graft toe seam. Block lightly to measurements. ■

Gauge
22 sts and 28 rows to 4"/10cm over St st using size 6 (4mm) needles.
Take time to check gauge.

Fair Isle Beanie

Texture complements colorwork as Fair Isle motifs in warm autumn tones
are crowned with vertical ridges.

DESIGNED BY AMY MACEYKO, NATURAL STITCHES, PITTSBURGH, PA

Size
Adult Medium

Knitted Measurements
Brim circumference 21"/53cm

Materials
■ 1 1¾oz/50g hank (each approx
136yd/125m) of Cascade Yarns *Cascade
220 Sport* (wool) each in #2453 pumpkin
spice (A), #8021 beige (B), and #9408
cordovan (C)

■ Size 3 (3.25mm) circular needle,
16"/40.5cm long, *or size to obtain gauge*

■ One set (5) size 3 (3.25mm) double-
pointed needles (dpns)

■ Stitch markers

■ Tapestry needle

Beanie
With circular needle and A, cast on 150
sts. Join to work in the rnd, being careful
not to twist sts, and place marker (pm)
for beg of rnd.
Rnd 1 *K1 tbl, p1; rep from * to end
of rnd.
Rep rnd 1 for approx 1"/2.5cm.
Inc rnd *K8, M1; rep from * to last 6 sts,
k6—168 sts.
Knit 1 rnd, then work rnds 1–39 of chart.
With A, cont in St st until hat measures
approx 6¼"/15.9cm from cast-on.

Gauge
26 sts and 34 rows to 4"/10cm over St st using size 3 (3.25mm) needles.
Take time to check gauge.

Fair Isle Beanie

CROWN SHAPING

Rnds 1 and 2 [P2, k2 tbl, p10, k2 tbl, p7, k2 tbl, p5, k2 tbl, p7, k2 tbl, p10, k2 tbl, p3] 3 times.

Rnd 3 (dec) [P2, k1 tbl, k2tog tbl, p9, k1 tbl, k2tog tbl, p6, k1 tbl, k2tog tbl, p3, k2tog, k1 tbl, p6, k2tog, k1 tbl, p9, k2tog, k1 tbl, p3] 3 times—150 sts.

Rnd 4 [P2, k2 tbl, p9, k2 tbl, p6, k2 tbl, p3, k2 tbl, p6, k2 tbl, p9, k2 tbl, p3] 3 times.

Rnd 5 (dec) [P2, k1 tbl, k2tog tbl, p8, k1 tbl, k2tog tbl, p5, k1 tbl, k2tog tbl, p1, k2tog, k1 tbl, p5, k2tog,k1 tbl, p8, k2tog, k1 tbl, p3] 3 times—132 sts.

Rnd 6 [P2, k2 tbl, p8, k2 tbl, p5, k2 tbl, p1, k2 tbl, p5, k2 tbl, p8, k2 tbl, p3] 3 times.

Rnd 7 (dec) [P2, k1 tbl, k2tog tbl, p7, k1 tbl, k2tog tbl, p4, k1 tbl, S2KP, k1 tbl, p4, k2tog, k1 tbl, p7, k2tog, k1 tbl, p3] 3 times—114 sts.

Rnd 8 [P2, k2 tbl, p7, k2 tbl, p4, k3 tbl, p4, k2 tbl, p7, k2 tbl, p3] 3 times.

Rnd 9 (dec) [P2, k1 tbl, k2tog tbl, p6, k1 tbl, k2tog tbl, p3, S2KP, p3, k2tog, k1 tbl, p6, k2tog, k1 tbl, p3] 3 times—96 sts.

Rnd 10 [P2, k2 tbl, p6, k2 tbl, p7, k2 tbl, p6, k2 tbl, p3] 3 times.

Rnd 11 (dec) [P2, k1 tbl, K2tog tbl, p5, k1 tbl, k2tog tbl, p1, p3tog, p1, K2tog, k1 tbl, p5, k2tog, k1 tbl, p3] 3 times—78 sts.

Rnd 12 [P2, k2 tbl, p5, k2 tbl, p3, k2 tbl, p5, k2 tbl, p3] 3 times.

Rnd 13 (dec) [P2tog, k1 tbl, k2tog tbl, p4, k1 tbl, k2tog tbl, p1, k2tog, k1 tbl, p4, k2tog, k1 tbl, p2tog, p1] 3 times—60 sts.

Rnd 14 [P1, k2 tbl, p4, k2 tbl, p1, k2 tbl, p4, k2 tbl, p2] 3 times.

Rnd 15 [P1, k1 tbl, k2tog tbl, p3, k1 tbl, s2kp, k1 tbl, p3, k2tog, k1 tbl, p2] 3 times—48 sts.

Rnd 16 (dec) [P1, k1 tbl, k2tog tbl, p2, s2kp, p2, k2tog, k1 tbl, p2] 3 times—36 sts.

Rnd 17 (dec) P1, [k1 tbl, k2tog tbl, p3, k2tog, k1 tbl, p3tog] 3 times (last p3tog will include 1st st of next rnd)—24 sts.

Rnd 18 (dec) [S2KP, p1] 6 times—12 sts. Cut yarn, leaving a 6"/15.2cm tail. Thread tail through rem sts, pull tightly to secure.

Finishing

Block lightly to measurements. ∎

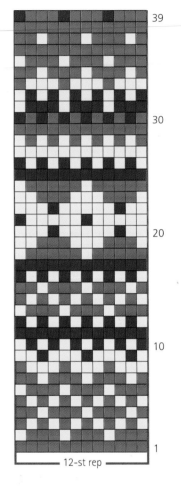

Color Key

- Pumpkin spice (A)
- Beige (B)
- Cordovan (C)

26

Felted Handbag

A bright color, elegant shape, and handy button closure make this take-anywhere purse an instant classic.

DESIGNED BY ERICA KEMPF BROUGHTON, NOMAD YARNS, PLAINFIELD, IN

◼◼☐☐

Knitted Measurements

BEFORE FELTING:
Width 19"/48cm
Height 9"/23cm
Depth 3½"/9cm
Handle length 17½"/44.5cm

AFTER FELTING:
Width 15"/38cm
Height 5"/12.5cm
Depth 2½"/6cm
Handle length 16"/40.5cm

Materials

◼ 2 3½oz/100g hanks (each approx 220yd/106m) of Cascade Yarns *Cascade 220 Heathers* (wool) in #9488 Christmas red heather

◼ One set (5) size 10½ (6.5mm) double-pointed needles (dpns) *or size to obtain gauge*

◼ Stitch holders or waste yarn

◼ Button or felt bauble (for closure)

3-Needle Bind-Off

1) Hold right sides of pieces together on two needles. Insert third needle knitwise into first st of each needle, and wrap yarn knitwise.
2) Knit these two sts together, and slip them off the needles. *Knit the next two sts together in the same manner.
3) Slip first st on 3rd needle over 2nd st and off needle. Rep from * in step 2 across row until all sts are bound off.

Handbag

Cast on 62 sts. Work 26 rows in St st to form bottom of bag.
Do not bind off. Pick up and k 13 sts along short side, 62 sts along opposite long side, and 13 sts along rem short side—150 sts. Join to work in the rnd and place marker (pm) for beg of rnd.
Rnds 1–14 Knit.
Rnd 15 *K2tog, k13; rep from * to end of rnd—140 sts.
Rnds 16–25 Knit.
Rnd 26 *K2tog, K12; rep from * to end of rnd—130 sts.
Rnds 27–36 Knit.
Rnd 37 *K2tog, K11; rep from * to end of rnd—120 sts.
Rnds 38–47 Knit.
Rnd 48 *K2tog, k10; rep from * to end of rnd—110 sts.
Rnds 49 and 50 Knit.
Next rnd Bind off 38 sts, k17 and place these 17 sts on holder, bind off 12 sts, k14 and place these 14 sts on holder, bind off 12 sts, k17. Work handle over these 17 sts.

Gauge
14 sts and 18 rows to 4"/10cm over St st using size 10½ (6.5mm) needles.
Take time to check gauge.

26 Felted Handbag

HANDLE
Rows 1 and 2 K17.
Row 3 K7, SK2P, k7—15 sts.
Rows 4 and 5 Knit.
Row 6 K6, SK2P, k6—13 sts.
Rows 7 and 8 Knit.
Row 9 K5, SK2P, k5—11 sts.
Place these 11 sts on a holder. Place other 17 sts from holder on needles and rep rows 1–9. Knit these 11 sts every row until handle measures approx 17½"/44.5cm long. Making sure handle isn't twisted, join to held 11 sts using 3-needle bind-off.

BUTTON TAB
Place 14 sts from holder back on needles. Knit every row until tab measures approx 3"/7.5cm long.
Row 1 K5, k2tog, [yo] twice, k2tog, k5.
Row 2 K6, k1 in first yo, p1 in second yo, k6.
Rows 3 and 4 Knit.
Row 5 Ssk, k to last 2 sts, k2tog—2 sts dec.
Rep row 5 until 4 sts rem. Bind off.

Finishing
Weave in ends. Felt by machine as foll:
1) Use a low water setting and hottest temperature in a top-loading washing machine. Add small amount of laundry detergent and jeans or towels for agitation.
2) Place item in a lingerie bag or zippered pillowcase and add to machine. Check the felting progress frequently, removing item when the individual stitches are no longer visible and item is felted to the desired size.
3) Place item in cool water to stop the felting process and remove suds. Remove from lingerie bag and roll gently in towel to remove excess water.
4) Block and shape while wet. Pin into shape or stuff with plastic bags, and allow to air dry completely.
Sew on button or felt ball as desired opposite buttonhole. ■

Welted Pine Tree Beanie

You can almost smell the pine needles! This unisex hat with a colorwork band would make a great holiday gift.

DESIGNED BY BECKY CURRAN, REDLANDS YARN COMPANY, REDLANDS, CA

Sizes

Instructions are written for Adult Small/Medium. Changes for Large/X-Large are in parentheses.

Knitted Measurements

Brim circumference 20 (22)"/51 (56)cm

Materials

- 1 3½oz/100g ball (each approx 220yd/201m) of Cascade Yarns *220 Superwash* (superwash wool) each in #1920 pumpkin spice (A), #1919 turtle (B), and #1926 doeskin heather (C)
- Size 7 (4.5mm) circular needle, 16"/41cm long, *or size to obtain gauge*
- One set (5) size 7 (4.5mm) double-pointed needles (dpns)
- Stitch markers

Notes

1) Change to dpns when sts no longer comfortably fit on circular needle.
2) Slip all sts purlwise.

Beanie

With circular needle and A, cast on 99 (110) sts. Join to work in the rnd, being careful not to twist sts, and place marker (pm) for beg of rnd. (This marker should be a different color from the others.)

Rnds 1–3 Purl.

Rnds 4–6 Knit.

Rnds 7–9 Purl.

Break A, leaving a 6"/15cm tail.

Rnd 10 With C, knit.

Rnd 11 Purl, pm after every 11 sts.

Rnd 12 With B, *sl 1 wyib, (k1, sl 1 wyib) 5 times; rep from * to end of rnd.

Rnd 13 *Sl 1 wyib, (p1, sl 1 wyib) 5 times; rep from * to end of rnd.

Rnd 14 With C, *k5, sl 1 wyib, k5; rep from * to end of rnd.

Rnd 15 *P5, sl 1 wyib, p5; rep from * to end of rnd.

Rnd 16 With B, *sl 2 wyib, k7, sl 2 wyib; rep from * to end of rnd.

Rnd 17 *Sl 2 wyib, p7, sl 2 wyib; rep from * to end of rnd.

Rnd 18 With C, *k3, sl 2 wyib, k1, sl 2 wyib, k3; rep from * to end of rnd.

Rnd 19 *P3, sl 2 wyib, p1, sl 2 wyib, p3; rep from * to end of rnd.

Rnd 20 With B, *sl 3 wyib, k5, sl 3 wyib; rep from * to end of rnd.

Rnd 21 *Sl 3 wyib, p5, sl 3 wyib; rep from * to end of rnd.

Rnd 22 With C, *k4, sl 1 wyib, k1, sl 1 wyib, k4; rep from * to end of rnd.

Rnd 23 *P4, sl 1 wyib, p1, sl 1 wyib, p4; rep from * to end of rnd.

Rnd 24 With B, *sl 1 wyib, k1, sl 2 wyib, k3, sl 2 wyib, k1, sl 1 wyib; rep from * to end of rnd.

Rnd 25 *Sl 1 wyib, p1, sl 2 wyib, p3, sl 2 wyib, p1, sl 1 wyib; rep from * to end of rnd.

Rnd 26 Rep rnd 14.

Rnd 27 Rep rnd 15.

Gauge

19 sts and 26 rows to 4"/10cm over St st using size 7 (4.5mm) needles.
Take time to check gauge.

Welted Pine Tree Beanie

Rnd 28 Rep rnd 12.
Rnd 29 Rep rnd 13.
Break B, leaving a 6"/15cm tail.
Rnd 30 With C, knit.
Rnd 31 Purl.
Break C, leaving a 6"/15cm tail.
Rnd 32 With A, knit.
Rnds 33–50 Rep rnds 1–6 three times.

CROWN SHAPING
Rnd 1 *P to 2 sts before marker, p2tog; rep from * to end of rnd—90 (100) sts.
Rnd 2 Purl.
Rnd 3 *P to 2 sts before marker, p2tog; rep from * to end of rnd—81 (90) sts.

Rnd 4 Knit.
Rnd 5 *K to 2 sts before marker, k2tog; rep from * to end of rnd—72 (80) sts.
Rnd 6 Knit.
Rnd 7 *P to 2 sts before marker, p2tog; rep from * to end of rnd—63 (70) sts.
Rnd 8 Purl.
Rnd 9 *P to 2 sts before marker, p2tog; rep from * to end of rnd—54 (60) sts.
Rnd 10 Knit.
Rnd 11 *K to 2 sts before marker, K2tog; rep from * to end of rnd—45 (50) sts.
Rnd 12 Knit.
Rnd 13 *P to 2 sts before marker, p2tog; rep from * to end of rnd—36 (40) sts.
Rnd 14 Purl.
Rnd 15 *P to 2 sts before marker, p2tog; rep from * to end of rnd—27 (30) sts.
Rnd 16 Knit.
Rnd 17 *K to 2 sts before marker, k2tog; rep from * to end of rnd—18 (20) sts.
Rnd 18 Knit.
Rnd 19 P2tog to end of rnd—9 (10) sts.

Finishing
Break yarn, leaving a 12"/30.5cm tail. Thread through rem sts. Pull tog tightly and secure end.
Block lightly to expand welted pattern. ■

Striped Dress

A striped skirt is set off by sweet bands of slipped stitches on this darling little-girl dress.

DESIGNED BY ELAINE ESKESEN, PINE TREE YARNS, DAMARISCOTTA, ME

Sizes
Instructions are written for 6 months. Changes for 12, 18, and 24 months are in parentheses.

Knitted Measurements
Chest circumference 18½ (19½, 20½, 21½)"/47 (49.5, 52, 54.5)cm
Length 11 (12, 12¾, 14)"/28 (30.5, 32.5, 35.5)cm
Circumference at hemline 24 (26½, 27, 29½)"/61 (67.5, 68.5, 75)cm

Materials
■ 2 3½oz/100g balls (each approx 220yd/201m) of Cascade Yarns *220 Superwash* (superwash wool) in #836 pink ice (A)
■ 1 ball in #871 white (B)
■ One pair size 6 (4mm) needles *or size to obtain gauge*
■ Size 6 (4mm) circular needle, 24"/60cm long
■ Stitch marker
■ Stitch holders
■ Four buttons, ¾"/19mm diameter

Ribbon Band Pattern
(multiple of 4 sts)
Rnds 1 and 3 With B, knit.
Rnd 2 With B, purl.
Rnds 4–6 With A, *k3, sl 1; rep from * around.
Rnd 7 With B, knit.
Rnd 8 With B, purl.

Stripe Pattern
Rnds 1–4 With A, knit.
Rnds 5–8 With B, knit.
Rep rnds 1–8 for stripe pat.

Note
Dress is worked in one piece to armholes.

Dress
SKIRT
With circular needle and A, cast on 120 (132, 136, 148) sts. Join to work in the rnd, taking care not to twist sts, and place marker (pm) for beg of rnd.
Rnds 1–8 Knit.
Rnd 9 (picot rnd) *K2tog, yo; rep from * to end of rnd.
Rnds 10–13 Knit.
Rnds 14–21 Work ribbon band pat to end of rnd.
Starting with rnd 1 of stripe pat, work until piece measures approx 7¾ (7¾, 9, 9)"/19.5 (19.5, 23, 23)cm from picot rnd, ending with rnd 4 of stripe pat.
Next rnd With A, *k2tog, k2; rep from * to end of rnd—90 (99, 102, 111) sts.
Next rnd With A, knit, dec 2 (3, 2, 3) sts evenly around—88 (96, 100, 108) sts.

Gauge
20 sts and 28 rnds to 4"/10cm over St st using size 6 (4mm) needles.
Take time to check gauge.

81

Striped Dress

BODICE

Rnds 1–8 Work ribbon band pat to end. Break B and cont in A only.
Rnds 9–11 Knit.
Rnd 12 Knit to last 2 sts.

DIVIDE FOR FRONT AND BACK

Next rnd Bind off last 2 sts of previous rnd and first 2 sts of next rnd, k40 (44, 46, 50), place these sts on holder for front, bind off next 4 sts, knit rem 40 (44, 46, 50) sts for back.

Back

Beg working back and forth in rows.
Next row (WS) K4, purl to last 4 sts, k4.
Next row Knit.
Rep last 2 rows until armhole measures 2½ (3, 3½, 4)"/6.5 (7.5, 9, 10)cm, ending with a WS row. Work 4 rows in garter st (knit every row).

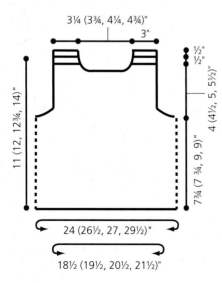

3¼ (3¾, 4¼, 4¾)"
3"
½"
½"
4 (4½, 5, 5½)"
11 (12, 12¾, 14)"
7¾ (7 ¾, 9, 9)"
24 (26½, 27, 29½)"
18½ (19½, 20½, 21½)"

LEFT BACK NECK AND SHOULDER SHAPING

Next row (RS) K25 (29, 31, 35), placing last 10 (14, 16, 20) sts just worked on holder for center front, k15.
Next row (WS) K2tog, knit to end of row—14 sts. Work on these sts only.
Next row Knit.
Rep last 2 rows twice more—12 sts. Knit 13 rows, ending with a WS row. Break yarn. Leave sts on spare needle.

RIGHT BACK NECK AND SHOULDER SHAPING

Return to 15 sts on needle for right back, ready for a WS row.
Next row (WS) Knit to last 2 sts, k2tog—14 sts.
Next row Knit.
Rep last 2 rows twice more—12 sts. Knit 13 rows, ending with a WS row.
Next row (RS) K12 from right shoulder, pick up and k 10 sts evenly along right front neck edge, k10 (14, 16, 20) from center front holder, pick up and k 10 sts evenly along left front neck edge, k 12 from left shoulder—54 (58, 60, 64) sts. Bind off.

Front

Place 40 (44, 46, 50) sts from front holder on needle, ready for a WS row.
Next row (WS) K4, purl to last 4 sts, k4.
Next row Knit.
Rep last 2 rows until armhole measures 2½ (3, 3½, 4)"/6.5 (7.5, 9, 10)cm, ending with a WS row. Work 4 rows in garter st.

RIGHT FRONT NECK AND SHOULDER SHAPING

Next row (RS) K25 (29, 31, 35), placing last 10 (14, 16, 20) sts just worked on holder for center front, k15.
Next row (WS) K2tog, knit to end of row—14 sts. Cont working on these sts only.
Next row Knit.
Rep last 2 rows twice more—12 sts. Knit 9 rows, ending with a WS row.
Next (buttonhole) row (RS) K2, yo, k2tog, k4, yo, k2tog, k2.
Knit 3 rows, ending with a WS row. Break yarn. Leave sts on spare needle.

LEFT FRONT NECK AND SHOULDER SHAPING

Return to 15 sts on needle for right back, ready for a WS row.
Next row (WS) Knit to last 2 sts, k2tog—14 sts.
Next row Knit.
Rep last 2 rows twice more—12 sts. Knit 9 rows, ending with a WS row.
Next (buttonhole) row (RS) K2, yo, k2tog, k4, yo, k2tog, k2.
Knit 3 rows, ending with a WS row.
Next row (RS) K12 from left shoulder, pick up and k 10 sts evenly along left front neck edge, k10 (14, 16, 20) from center front holder, pick up and k 10 sts evenly along right front neck edge, k12 from right shoulder—54 (58, 60, 64) sts. Bind off.

Finishing

Block lightly. Sew buttons to back shoulders, approx ½"/1.5cm from bound-off edge, opposite buttonholes. Fold cast-on edge to WS along picot row and slip st in place to WS. ∎

Swirl Beret

A contrast cabled band and topknot are the perfect accents for a swirl of variegated color.

DESIGNED BY KATHY ZOLA, ELISSA'S CREATIVE WAREHOUSE, NEEDHAM, MA

Size
Woman's Medium

Knitted Measurements
Brim circumference 21"/53cm
Diameter (flat, at widest point)
10"/25.5cm

Materials

■ 1 3½oz/100g hank (each approx 220yd/201m) of Cascade Yarns *220 Superwash Paints* (superwash wool) in #9770 Celtic (A)

■ 1 1¾oz/50g hank (each approx 137yd/125m) of Cascade Yarns *220 Superwash Sport* (superwash merino) in #845 denim (B)

■ Size 6 (4mm) circular needle, 16"/41cm long, *or size to obtain gauge*

■ One pair of size 6 (4mm) needles

■ One set (5) size 6 (4mm) double-pointed needles (dpns)

■ Cable needle (cn)

■ Stitch markers

I-Cord
*Knit one row. Without turning work, slide the sts back to the opposite end of needle to work next row from RS. Pull yarn tightly from the end of the row. Rep from * to desired length.

Beret
With straight needles and A, cast on 11 sts.
Row 1 Sl 1 knitwise, k4, p1, k5.
Row 2 Sl 1 purlwise, p4, k1, p5.

Gauges
24 sts and 36 rows to 4"/10cm over St st using size 6 (4mm) needles.
24 sts and 20 rows to 4"/10cm over pat st using size 6 (4mm) needles.
Take time to check gauges.

Swirl Beret

Row 6 Sl 1 purlwise, p4, k1, p5.
Rep rows 1–6 until cable band measures 20"/51cm.
Bind off and graft ends of band together. With circular needle and loops formed by slipped sts at beg of each row, pick up and k 90 sts evenly spaced around 1 edge of band. Join to work in the rnd, place marker (pm) for beg of rnd.
Set-up row *[Yo, k1] 15 times, pm; rep from * to end of rnd—180 sts.
Pat row *[Yo, k2tog] 15 times, sl marker; rep from * to end of rnd.
Rep pat row 19 times more.

CROWN SHAPING
Note Change to dpns when sts no longer comfortably fit on circular needle.
Row 1 [*Yo, k2tog; rep from * until 4 sts rem before 1st marker, yo, k2tog, k2tog, sl marker] 6 times—172 sts.
Row 2 [*Yo, k2tog; rep from * until 4 sts rem before 1st marker, yo, k3tog, sl marker] 6 times—166 sts.
Row 3 Rep row 1—160 sts.
Row 4 Rep row 2—154 sts.
Rep rows 1 and 2 until 12 sts rem.

I-CORD TAIL
With B, k2tog to end of rnd—6 sts.
Work I-cord on 6 sts until tail measures 6"/15cm. Bind off.

Finishing
Fold cable band in half, WS tog, and loosely sew edges tog to form a casing. Block beret over a 10" plate.
Tie I-cord tail into a loose knot. ■

Row 3 Sl 1 knitwise, sl 2 to cn and hold to *front*, k2 from LH needle, k2 from cn, p1, sl 2 to cn and hold to *back*, k2 from LH needle, k2 from cn, k1.
Row 4 Sl 1 purlwise, p4, k1, p5.
Row 5 Sl 1 knitwise, k4, p1, k5.

Snowflake Mittens

Tradition meets technique in these Nordic-inspired mittens with a Fair Isle snowflake motif.

DESIGNED BY TRISH MITBERG, KNITTING BEE, PORTLAND, OR

Size
Woman's Medium

Knitted Measurements
Hand circumference 7"/18cm
Length to middle fingertip 10"/25.5cm

Materials
- 1 3½oz/100g hank (each approx 220yd/201m) of Cascade Yarns *Cascade 220* (wool) each in #8415 cranberry (MC) and #8021 beige (CC)
- One set (5) each sizes 5 and 6 (3.75 and 4mm) double-pointed needles (dpns) *or size to obtain gauge*
- Stitch markers
- Tapestry needle

Stitch Glossary
M1R Insert LH needle from back to front under the strand between last st worked and next st on LH needle. K into front loop to twist st.
M1L Insert LH needle from front to back under the strand between last st worked and next st on LH needle. K into back loop to twist st.

Mittens (make 2)
With larger needles and MC, cast on 40 sts, divide evenly among 4 dpns. Join, being careful not to twist sts, and place marker (pm) for beg of rnd.
Rnd 1 Purl.
Rnd 2 Knit.
Rnds 3–17 *With MC, k1; with CC, k1; rep from * to end of rnd.
Rnds 18 and 19 With MC, knit.
Rnds 20 and 22 *With MC, k1; with CC, k1; rep from * to end of rnd.
Rnd 21 *With CC, k1; with MC, k1; rep from * to end of rnd. Break CC and cont in MC. Change to smaller needles.

THUMB GUSSET
Note Beg-of-rnd marker will mark left side of gusset increases.
Rnd 23 K40, pm, M1L, slip marker (sm)— 41 sts.
Rnds 24 and 25 Knit.
Rnd 26 K40, sm, M1R, k to next marker, M1L, sm—43 sts.
Rnds 27 and 28 Knit.
Rep last 3 rnds 4 times more—51 sts.

Snowflake Mittens

Rnd 41 K40, remove marker and place 11 thumb sts on holder. Remove beg of rnd marker. Cast on 1 st, place new beg of rnd marker, cast on 1 st—42 sts. Join to cont working in the rnd.

Rnd 42 Knit. Change to larger needles.

Rnd 43 Join CC, [work rnd 1 of chart over next 21 sts] twice.

Cont as now est, working rows 2–19 of chart. Break CC and cont in MC. Change to smaller needles.

Rnd 62 Knit.

Rnd 63 [K1, ssk, k15, k2tog, k1] twice—38 sts.

Rnd 64 Knit.

Rnd 65 [K1, ssk, k13, k2tog, k1] twice—34 sts.

Rnd 66 Knit.

Rnd 67 [K1, ssk, k11, k2tog, k1] twice—30 sts.

Rnd 68 [K1, ssk, k9, k2tog, k1] twice—26 sts.

Rnd 69 [K1, ssk, k7, k2tog, k1] twice—22 sts.

Rnd 70 [K1, ssk, k5, k2tog, k1] twice—18 sts.

Rnd 71 [K1, ssk, k3, k2tog, k1] twice—14 sts.

Rnd 72 [K1, ssk, k1, k2tog, k1] twice—10 sts.

Break yarn, leaving 8"/20cm tail. Thread through rem sts and pull tightly to secure.

THUMB

Place 11 sts from thumb holder onto smaller dpns, divded evenly among 4 needles.

Rnd 1 With MC, pick up and k 4 sts along gap created by 2 sts cast on, k the 11 held sts, pm and join for working in the rnd—15 sts.

Rnds 2–14 Knit.

Rnd 15 *K1, k2tog; rep from * to end of rnd—10 sts.

Rnd 16 Knit.

Rnd 17 [K2tog] 5 times—5 sts.

Break yarn, leaving 6"/15cm tail. Thread through rem sts and pull tightly to secure.

Finishing

Block lightly to measurements. ■

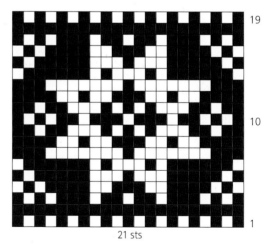

21 sts

Color Key

■ Cranberry (MC)

☐ Beige (CC)

Acorn Hat

What better way to warm up an autumn baby than with this adorable, quick-to-knit cap?

DESIGNED BY RONDA HATTORI, MAIN ST. YARN SHOP, HARTFORD, WI

Size
Infant, 0–6 months

Knitted Measurements
Circumference 18"/45.5cm
Length 6½"/16.5cm

Materials
- 1 3½oz/100g hank (each approx 220yd/201m) of Cascade Yarns *220 Superwash* (superwash wool) each in #858 dark ginger (MC) and #853 butterscotch (CC)
- One each sizes 9 and 10 (5.5 and 6mm) circular needle, 16"/40cm long, *or size to obtain gauge*
- One set (5) size 10 (6mm) double-pointed needles (dpns)
- Stitch marker
- Tapestry needle

Stitch Glossary
Kfb Knit into front and back of next st— 1 st increased.

Seed Stitch
(over an even number of sts)
Rnd 1 *K1, p1; rep from * around.
Rnd 2 K the purl and p the knit sts.
Rep rnd 2 for seed st.

Notes
1) Hat is worked with 2 strands of yarn held together throughout.
2) Change to dpns when there are too few sts to fit comfortably on circular needle.

Hat
With smaller circular needle and 2 strands of CC held together, cast on 48 stitches.

Join to work in the round, being careful not to twist sts, and place marker for beg of rnd. Work in seed st for 1¼"/3cm. Break CC and join 2 strands of MC.
Next rnd Knit. Change to larger circular needle.
Next (inc) rnd *K1, kfb; rep from * around—72 sts.
Cont even in St st (k every round) until hat measures 4½"/11.5cm from beg.

CROWN SHAPING
Rnd 1 *K2, ssk, k2tog, k2; rep from * around—54 sts.
Rnds 2 and 3 Knit.
Rnd 4 *K1, ssk, k2tog, k1; rep from * around—36 sts.
Rnds 5 and 6 Knit.
Rnd 7 *Ssk, k2tog; repeat from * around—18 sts.
Rnd 8 *K2tog; rep from * around—9 sts.
Rnd 9 [K2tog] 4 times, k1—5 sts. Break MC and join 2 strands of CC.

Finishing
I-CORD TOP
Next rnd *K5 onto one dpn. Do not turn. Slide sts to beg of needle. Rep from * until I-cord measures 1½"/4cm. Break yarn, leaving a long tail. Thread through rem sts and pull tightly to secure. Block lightly to measurements. ∎

Gauge
16 sts and 20 rnds to 4"/10cm over St st with 2 strands of yarn held tog using size 10 (6mm) needles. *Take time to check gauge.*

Slip Stitch Mittens

Cabled cuffs and a two-color slip stitch pattern come together in a cozy interplay of color and texture.

DESIGNED BY SUZY ALLEN, THE VILLAGE KNITTER, BABYLON, NY

Size
Woman's Small/Medium

Knitted Measurements
Hand circumference 8"/20cm
Hand length 6½"/16.5cm
Cuff length 3¼"/8cm

Materials
■ 1 3½oz/100g hank (approx 220yd/201m) of Cascade Yarns *Cascade 220* (wool) each in #9427 duck egg blue (A) and #9419 Vermeer blue (B)
■ One set (5) size 7 (4.5mm) double-pointed needles (dpns) *or size to obtain gauge*
■ Cable needle (cn)
■ Stitch holder

Stitch Glossary
3-st RPC Sl 1 st to cn, hold to *back*; k2, p1 from cn.
3-st LPC Sl 2 sts to cn, hold to *front*; p1, k2 from cn.
Kfb Knit into the front and back of next st—1 st increased.

Slip Stitch Pattern
(over an even number of sts)
Rnds 1 and 2 With A, knit.
Rnd 3 With B, k1, *sl 1 wyib, sl 1 wyif; rep from * to last st, sl 1 wyib.
Rnd 4 With B, *sl 1 wyif, sl 1 wyib; repeat from * to end of rnd.
Rnds 5 and 6 With A, knit.
Rnd 7 With B, sl 1 wyib, k1, *sl 1 wyib, sl 1 wyif; repeat from * to end of rnd.
Rnd 8 With B, *sl 1 wyib, sl 1 wyif; repeat from * to end of rnd.
Repeat rnds 1–8 for slip st pat.

Note
The cuff is worked flat; then the rest of the mitten is worked in the round.

Mitten (make 2)
With A, cast on 38 sts.
Rows 1–3 Knit.
Row 4 (RS) P4, 3-st RPC, *p3, 3-st RPC; rep from * to last st, p1.
Row 5 (WS) K2, *p2, k4; rep from * to end.
Row 6 *P3, 3-st RPC; rep from * to last 2 sts, p2.
Row 7 K3, p2, *k4, p2; rep from * to last 3 sts, k3.
Row 8 P2, *3-st RPC, p3; rep from * to end.
Row 9 *K4, p2; rep from * to last 2 sts, k2.
Row 10 P1, *3-st RPC, p3; rep from * to last st, p1.
Row 11 K5, p2, *k4, p2; rep from * to last st, k1.
Row 12 P1, *3-st LPC, p3; rep from * to last st, p1.
Row 13 *K4, p2; rep from * to last 2 sts, k2.
Row 14 P2, *3-st LPC, p3; rep from * to end.

Gauge
18 sts and 24 rows to 4"/10cm over St st using size 7 (4.5mm) needles.
Take time to check gauge.

Slip Stitch Mittens

Row 15 K3, p2, *k4, p2; rep from * to last 3 sts, k3.
Row 16 *P3, 3-st LPC; rep from * to last 2 sts, p2.
Row 17 K2, *p2, k4; rep from * to end.
Row 18 P4, 3-st LPC, *p3; 3-st LPC, rep from * to last st, p1.
Row 19 K1, *p2, k4; rep from * to last st, k1.
Row 20 Purl.
Rows 21 and 22 Knit.

BEG HAND
With RS facing, join to work in the round. Place marker (pm) for beg of rnd.
Set-up rnd K17, k2tog, k17, k2tog—36 sts.
Work in slip st pat for 11 rows, beg with rnd 2 of pat.

GUSSET
Cont in pat as est, AT THE SAME TIME, work inc for thumb gusset as foll:

Inc rnd 1 Work to last 2 sts in est pat, pm, [kfb] twice—38 sts.
Inc rnd 2 Work in pat to marker, sl m, kfb, work to 1 st before marker, kfb—40 sts.
Work next 2 rnds in slip st pat as est. Rep inc rnd 2 twice (10 sts between markers). Work next 2 rnds in slip st pat as est.
Next rnd Work in pat as est to m, sl 10 sts onto holder, cast on 2 sts—36 sts.
Cont in pat as est until piece measures approx 6"/15cm from beg of slip st pat, ending with rnd 4 or 8 of pat.

TOP
Cont in pat as est, AT THE SAME TIME, work dec for top of hand as foll:
Rnd 1 K16, k2tog, pm, k16, k2tog.
Rnd 2 [K to 2 sts before m, k2tog] twice.
Rnds 3 and 4 Cont in slip st pat as est.
Rnds 5 and 6 Rep rnd 2.
Rep rnds 3–6 three times more.
Next rnd Work k2tog to end of rnd. Break yarn, leaving 10"/25cm tail.
Weave end through all sts and pull tight.

THUMB
With A, pick up and k 6 sts from body of mitten. Knit held gusset sts (16 sts total). Work in slip st pat, beg with rnd 2 of pat, until thumb measures approx 3"/7.5cm long, ending with rnd 2 or 6 of pat.
Next rnd K2tog to end of rnd. Break yarn, leaving 6"/15cm tail. Weave end through all sts and pull tight.

Finishing
Seam cuff. Block lightly to measurements. ▨

33

Sock Monkey Hat

Monkey around with your child in this adorable hat, finished with pompoms at the crown and on the earflap ties.

DESIGNED BY ERICA KEMPF BROUGHTON, NOMAD YARNS, PLAINFIELD, IN

◼◼◼▢

Size
Infant to 12 months

Knitted Measurements
Brim circumference 16"/40cm
Height (excluding earflaps) 6½"/16.5cm

Materials
■ 1 3½oz/100g ball (each approx 220 yd/201m) of Cascade Yarns *220 Superwash* (superwash wool) each in #1920 pumpkin spice (MC), #809 really red (A), and #910A winter white (B)

■ One set (5) size 6 (4mm) double-pointed needles (dpns) *or size to obtain gauge*

■ Size G/6 (4mm) crochet hook (optional)

■ Stitch markers, stitch holders

■ Small amount polyester fiberfill

■ Small amount worsted-weight black yarn

■ Pompom maker (optional)

■ Tapestry needle

Stitch Glossary
Kfb Knit into the front and back of next st—1 st increased.

Note
To avoid jog when changing colors, on second round of new color lift the first stitch of the round on the row below onto LH needle and knit together with first stitch.

Hat
With B, cast on 6 sts. Join to work in the rnd, taking care not to twist sts, and place marker (pm) for beg of rnd.
Rnd 1 and all odd-numbered rnds Knit.
Rnd 2 *Kfb; rep from * around—12 sts.
Rnd 4 Rep rnd 2—24 sts.
Rnd 6 (K1, kfb, pm) around—36 sts.
Rnd 8 (Knit to 1 st before marker, kfb) around—48 sts.
Rnd 9 Knit.
Rep last 2 rnds until there are 84 sts.
Rnds 15–17 Knit.
Change to A. Knit 3 rnds. Change to MC and work even until piece measures approx 5½"/14cm. Cont with MC, work in garter st (knit one rnd, purl one rnd) for 8 rnds, ending with a purl rnd.
Next rnd K20, bind off 26 sts, k20, place these 20 sts on holder, bind off rem 18 sts.

EAR FLAPS (MAKE 2)
Join MC and beg with WS row, work as foll over 20 sts:
Rows 1 and 2 Knit.
Row 3 K1, ssk, k to last 3 sts, k2tog, k1—2 sts dec.

Gauge
22 sts and 28 rows to 4"/10cm over St st using size 6 (4mm) needles.
Take time to check gauge.

Sock Monkey Hat

Rep rows 1–3 until 4 sts rem, then work rows 1 and 2 once more.
Next row Ssk, k2tog—2 sts.
Bind off. Break yarn, leaving 20"/51cm tail for braid.

MOUTH

With B, cast on 50 sts. Join to work in the round, taking care not to twist sts, and pm for beg of rnd.
Set-up rnd K19, pm, k6, pm, k19, pm, k6.
Rnd 1 *Sl marker, ssk, k to 2 sts before marker, k2tog; rep from * around—42 sts.
Rnd 2 and all even-numbered rnds Knit.
Rep last 2 rnds once more—34 sts.
Rnd 5 Sl marker, ssk, k to 2 sts before marker, k2tog, sl marker, k2tog, sl marker, ssk, knit to 2 sts before marker, k2tog, sl marker, k2tog—28 sts.
Change to B at beg of rnd 6.
Rnd 7 Sl marker, knit to 1 st before marker, [sl 1, remove marker] twice, k1, psso, knit to 1 st before marker, [sl 1, remove marker] twice, k1, psso—24 sts.
Rnds 8 and 9 Knit.
Sl first 12 sts onto 1st needle and last 12 sts onto 2nd needle. With black yarn, graft tog using Kitchener st.

Ears (make 2)

With MC, cast on 20 sts. Join to work in the rnd, taking care not to twist sts, and pm for beg of rnd.
Rnd 1 K10, pm, k10.

Rnd 2 [Sl marker, ssk, k to 2 sts before marker, k2tog] twice—16 sts.
Rnd 3 Knit.
Rep rnds 2 and 3 until 4 sts rem. Graft ears tog using Kitchener stitch.

Finishing

Stuff mouth loosely with fiberfill and sew onto front of hat with B. Make sure to sew the face onto the front of the hat (wider opening between earflaps).
Sew ears on sides of head with MC.
With black yarn, embroider French knots for eyes. If desired, with B and crochet hook, work 1 rnd of single crochet around lower edge of hat; or, alternately, whipstitch using a tapestry needle.

BRAIDS

Cut 40"/101cm lengths of MC and A, and draw through point of each earflap using a tapestry needle. Pull even. Braid all strands tog and tie securely.

POMPOMS

With B, make three 2"/5cm pompoms. Sew one to top of hat, and one to end of each braid. ∎

FRENCH KNOT

Twisted Stitch Mittens

A delicate allover mini-cable pattern gives these mittens
both a snug fit and a warm and thick fabric.

DESIGNED BY PHYLLIS ROWLEY, CLOSE KNIT, WYCKOFF, NJ

Size
Woman's Medium

Knitted Measurements
Hand circumference (not stretched)
6"/15cm
Length 10"/25cm

Materials
■ 2 1½oz/50g hanks
(each approx 137yd/125m)
of Cascade Yarns
220 Superwash Sport
(superwash merino) in
#1910 summer sky heather

■ One set (5) size 3 (3.25mm)
double-pointed needles (dpns)
or size to obtain gauge

■ Waste yarn

■ Tapestry needle

Stitch Glossary
RT K2tog and leave on LH needle, then
insert RH needle between the 2 sts just k
tog and k the first st again, then sl both
sts from LH needle.

Cable Pattern
Rnds 1 and 2 *K2, p2; rep from * to end
of rnd.
Rnd 3 *RT, p2; rep from * to end of round.
Repeat rnds 1–3 for cable pat.

Note
Left and right mittens are the same.

Mitten (make 2)
Cast on 52 stitches. Arrange over 3 dpns so
there are 20 sts on 1st needle, 20 sts on
2nd needle, 12 sts on 3rd needle.
Join to work in the rnd, being careful not to
twist sts, and place marker for beg of rnd.
Work cable pat for 5"/12.5cm, ending
with rnd 3.
At start of next rnd, set aside sts for
thumb as foll: [K2, p2] twice with waste
yarn. Sl those sts back to LH needle and
work again with working yarn.
Cont in cable pat as est until piece
measures approx 10"/25cm from cast-on
edge, ending with rnd 3.

MITTEN TOP
Rnd 1 *K2, p2tog; rep from * to end of
rnd.
Rnd 2 *K2, p1; rep from * to end of rnd.
Rnd 3 *K2tog, p1; rep from * to end of
rnd.
Rnd 4 K2tog around.
Break yarn, leaving 12"/30cm tail. Thread
tail through rem sts and pull tight,
securing end.

THUMB
Remove waste yarn and place 15 live sts
on 2 dpns. Starting with bottom sts,
work rnd 1 of cable pat, picking up 2 sts
at end of first needle and 3 sts at end of
second needle—20 sts. Cont to work in
pat as est until thumb measures approx
2½"/6cm.
Next rnd *K2tog, p2tog; rep from * to
end of rnd.
Next rnd K2tog around.
Break yarn, leaving 6"/15cm tail. Thread
tail though sts and pull tight, securing.

Finishing
Block lightly to measurements. ■

Gauge
22 sts and 30 rows to 4"/10cm over St st using size 3 (3.25mm) needles.
Take time to check gauge.

Column Cable Scarf

Twisted columns and seed stitch borders surround a central cable panel
for a striking interplay of textures.

DESIGNED BY BETTY BALCOMB, KNITTY CITY, NEW YORK, NY

Knitted Measurements
Width 8"/20.5cm
Length 60"/152.5cm

Materials
■ 3 3½oz/100g balls (each approx 220yd/201m) of Cascade Yarns *220 Superwash Paints* (superwash wool) in #9942 misty blue

■ One pair size 7 (4.5mm) needles *or size to obtain gauge*

■ Cable needle (cn)

Stitch Glossary
RT K2tog, do not sl off needle, k first st again, slip both sts off needle.
LT Knit the second st tbl, do not sl off needle, k first st, slip both sts off needle.
2-st RPC Slip 1 st to cn, hold to *back*, k1, p1 from cn.
2-st LPC Slip 1 st to cn, hold to *front*, p1, k1 from cn.

Seed Stitch
(over an odd number of sts)
Row 1 (RS) *K1, p1; rep from *, end k1.
Row 2 K the purl and p the knit sts.
Rep row 2 for seed st.

Scarf
With size 7 (4.5mm) needles, cast on 45 sts. Work in seed st until piece measures 1½"/4cm, end with a RS row.
Next row (WS) Work 5 sts in seed st, work next 35 sts in seed st, inc 7 sts evenly across, work 5 sts in seed st—52 sts.

BEG CHARTS
Next row (RS) Work 5 sts in seed st, work row 1 of chart 1 over next 11 sts, work row 1 of chart 2 over next 20 sts, work row 1 of chart 3 over next 11 sts, work 5 sts in seed st. Cont in pats as established, keeping first and last 5 sts in seed st and working appropriate row of each chart until rows 1–32 of chart 2 have been worked 12 times, end with a WS row.
Next row (RS) Work 5 sts in seed st, work row 1 of chart 1 over next 11 sts, work row 1 of chart 2 over next 20 sts, work row 1 of chart 3 over next 11 sts, work 5 sts in seed st.
Next row (WS) Work 5 sts in seed st, work row 2 of chart 3 over next 11 sts, work row 2 of chart 2 over next 20 sts, work row 2 of chart 1 over next 11 sts, work 5 sts in seed st.
Next row (RS) Work 5 sts in seed st, work next 42 sts in seed st, AT THE SAME TIME, dec 7 sts evenly over these 42 sts, work 5 sts in seed st—45 sts. Work in seed st over all sts for 1½"/4cm. Bind off in pat.

Finishing
Block lightly to measurements. ■

Gauge
20 sts and 26 rows to 4"/10cm over St st using size 7 (4.5mm) needles.
Take time to check gauge.

35
Column Cable Scarf

CHART 1

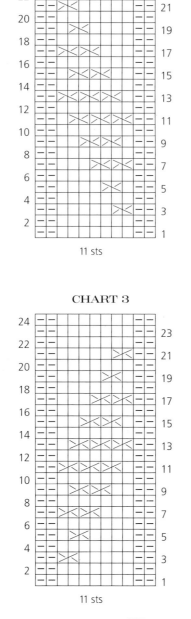

11 sts

CHART 3

11 sts

CHART 2

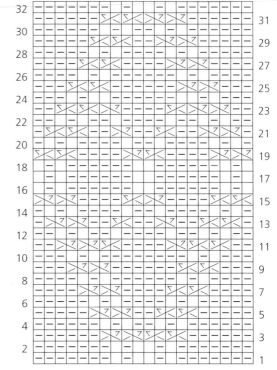

20 sts

Stitch Key

☐	K on RS, p on WS
—	P on RS, k on WS
⧖	LT
⧗	RT
⧖	2-st LPC
⧗	2-st RPC

36

Fair Isle Banded Hat

A sweet and simple diamond motif around the band is repeated at the top,
on a cute-as-a-button button cover.

DESIGNED BY DEB PETERSON, BLISS YARNS, BRENTWOOD, TN

Size
Woman's Small/Medium

Knitted Measurements
Brim circumference 19"/48cm
Height 8½"/21.5cm

Materials
■ 1 3½oz/100g ball (each approx
220yd/201m) of Cascade Yarns
Cascade 220 Heathers (wool)
each in #9332 sapphire (MC),
#9559 indigo frost heather (A),
and #4008 carmine heather (B)

■ Two size 7 (4.5mm) circular needles,
16"/40.5cm long, *or size to obtain gauge*

■ One set (5) size 7 (4.5mm) double-
pointed needles (dpns)

■ Size H/8 (5mm) crochet hook and scrap
yarn (for provisional cast-on)

■ Stitch markers

■ One flat non-shank button,
1–2"/2.5–5cm diameter

Provisional Cast-On
Using scrap yarn and crochet hook, ch
the number of sts to cast on plus a few
extra. Cut a tail and pull the tail through
the last chain. With knitting needle and
yarn, pick up and knit the stated number
of sts through the "purl bumps" on the
back of the chain. To remove waste
chain, when instructed, pull out the tail
from the last crochet stitch. Gently and
slowly pull on the tail to unravel the
crochet stitches, carefully placing each
released knit stitch on a needle.

Hat
FAIR ISLE BAND
With one circular needle and A, cast
on 96 sts using provisional cast-on.
Join to work in the rnd, taking care
not to twist sts, and place marker (pm)
for beg of rnd.
Work rnds 1–6 of chart 1 twice, and then
rnds 1–3 once more. Break MC and A,
leaving a 6"/15cm tail for each.
Carefully remove scrap yarn from cast-on
edge, placing live sts on 2nd circular
needle. Fold brim in half and, with B,
k2tog around, taking one corresponding
st from each needle—96 sts. Purl one
rnd. Break B.

BODY
Join MC.
Rnd 1 Knit.
Rnd 2 *K6, pm; rep from * to end of rnd.
Rnd 3 *Knit to marker, sl marker, M1; rep
from * to end of rnd—112 sts.
Rnd 4 Knit.
Rep rnds 3 and 4 twice more—144 sts.
Cont in St st, removing all markers, until
piece measures approx 2"/5cm from last
inc rnd.

Gauge
20 sts and 28 rows to 4"/10cm over St st using size 7 (4.5mm) needles.
Take time to check gauge.

Fair Isle Banded Hat

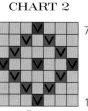

CHART 1

6-st rep

CHART 2

7 sts

Color Key

◼ Sapphire (MC)

▨ Indigo frost heather (A)

◼ Carmine heather (B)

V Duplicate stitch

CROWN SHAPING

Note Change to dpns when sts no longer comfortably fit on circular needle.
Rnd 1 *K16, pm; rep from * to end of rnd.
Rnd 2 *Knit to 2 sts before marker, k2tog, sl marker; rep from * to end of rnd—135 sts.
Rnd 3 Knit.
Rep rnds 2 and 3 until 9 sts rem.
Break yarn, leaving 10"/25cm tail. Thread tail through rem sts, pull tightly to secure.

Button Cover

With 2 dpns and A, cast on 7 sts.
Row 1 Purl.
Row 2 (RS) K1, M1; knit to last st, M1, k1—9 sts.
Row 3 Purl.
Rep rows 2 and 3 three times more—15 sts.
Work 3 rows even in St st, ending with RS row.
Row 13 (WS) P1, p2tog, purl to last 3 sts, p2tog, p1—13 sts.
Row 14 Knit.
Rep rows 13 and 14 three times more—7 sts. Bind off.
Following chart 2, work duplicate st with MC and B in center 7 rows of piece.

Finishing

Block lightly to measurements.
When fully dry, enclose button by sewing around all sides of button cover and pulling tight. Secure end, leaving long-enough tail to attach to hat. Sew button securely to top of hat. ◼

Eyelet Gauntlets

Drama takes center stage with a pair of flared wristers, edged with rows of eyelets.

DESIGNED BY RACHEL MAURER, LA CASITA YARN SHOP CAFÉ, BROOKLYN, NY

Sizes
Instructions are written for Woman's Small/Medium. Changes for Woman's Large are in parentheses.

Knitted Measurements
Wrist circumference 6 (7)"/15 (18)cm
Length 6½"/16.5cm

Materials
■ 1 3¾oz/100g hank (approx 220yd/201m) of Cascade Yarns *Cascade 220 Heathers* (wool) in #9453 amethyst heather (1 hank makes 2 pairs)

■ One set (5) size 7 (4.5mm) double-pointed needles (dpns)
or size to obtain gauge

■ Stitch markers

Stitch Glossary
Pfb Purl into front and back of next st—1 st increased.

Rib Pattern
(multiple of 4 sts)
Rnd 1 *K3, p1; rep from * to end of rnd.
Repeat rnd 1 for rib pat.

Gauntlet (make 2)
Cast on 32 (36) stitches. Join to work in the rnd, being careful not to twist sts. Place marker (pm) for beg of rnd.
Rnd 1 Knit.
Rnd 2 Purl.
Rnd 3 *Yo, k2tog; rep from * to end of rnd.
Rnd 4 Purl.
Rnd 5 Knit.
Rnds 6–18 Work rib pat.
Rnd 19 *K3, pfb; rep from * to end of rnd—40 (45) sts.
Rnds 20 and 21 *K3, p2; rep from * to end of rnd.
Rnd 22 *K3, p1, pfb; rep from * to end of rnd—48 (54) sts.
Rnds 23 and 24 *K3, p3; rep from * to end of rnd.
Rnd 25 *K3, pfb, p2; rep from * to end of rnd—56 (63) sts.
Rnds 26 and 27 *K3, p4 rep from * to end of rnd.
Rnd 28 *K3, p3, pfb; rep from * to end of rnd—64 (72) sts.
Rnds 29 and 30 *K3, p5; rep from * to end of rnd.
Rnd 31 *K3, pfb, p4; rep from * to end of rnd—72 (81) sts.
Rnds 32 and 33 *K3, p6; rep from * to end of rnd.
Rnd 34 *K3, p5, pfb; rep from * to end of rnd—80 (90) sts.
Rnds 35 and 36 *K3, p7; rep from * to end of rnd.
Rnd 37 Knit.
Rnd 38 Purl.
Rnd 39 *Yo, k2tog; rep from * to end of rnd.
Rnd 40 Purl.
Rnd 41 Knit.
Rnd 42 Bind off purlwise.

Finishing
Block lightly to measurements. ■

Gauge
20 sts and 24 rows to 4"/10cm in rib pat using size 7 (4.5mm) needles.
Take time to check gauge.

Fair Isle Hat & Mittens

Show your love for a new arrival with a tiny cap and mittens, encircled by a heart motif.

DESIGNED BY LAMBSPUN OF COLORADO, FORT COLLINS, CO

Size
Newborn to 3 months

Knitted Measurements
Hat circumference 10½"/26.5cm
Hat length 5½"/14cm
Mitten circumference 4½"/11.5cm
Mitten length 3½"/9cm

Materials
■ 1 3½oz/100g ball (each approx 220yd/201m) of Cascade Yarns *220 Superwash* (superwash wool) each in #836 pink ice (MC) and #850 lime sherbert (CC)

■ One set (5) each sizes 6 and 8 (4 and 5mm) double-pointed needles (dpns) *or size to obtain gauge*

■ Stitch markers

■ Tapestry needle

I-Cord
*With 2 dpns, knit one row. Without turning work, slide the sts back to the opposite end of needle to work next row from RS. Pull yarn tightly from the end of the row. Rep from * until desired length.

Modified Twisted Rib
Rnd 1 *K1, p1; rep from * to end of rnd.
Rnd 2 *K1 tbl, p1; rep from * to end of rnd.
Rep rnds 1 and 2 for modified twisted rib.

Hat
With smaller needles and MC, cast on 60 sts. Join to work in the rnd, being careful not to twist. Place marker (pm) for beg of rnd.
Work in modified twisted rib for approx 1"/2.5cm.
Change to larger needles and work in St st (knit every rnd) for 2 rnds.
Join CC and work rnds 1–10 of chart 1. Break CC, leaving 6"/15cm tail.
Cont in st st with MC until piece measures 4¼"/11cm from beg.

CROWN SHAPING
Rnd 1 *K2tog, k8; rep from * to end of rnd.
Rnd 2 *K2tog, k7; rep from * to end of rnd.
Cont as est, working 1 fewer st bet dec, until 12 sts rem.
Next 2 rnds K2tog to end of rnd—3 sts. Work I-cord with these 3 sts for 1½"/4cm. Break yarn, leaving 6"/15cm tail.

Mittens (make 2)
With MC and smaller needles, cast on 20 sts. Join to work in the rnd, being careful not to twist. Pm for beg of round.
Work in modified twisted rib for approx 1"/2.5cm. Change to larger needles.
Next rnd Inc 4 sts evenly around—24 sts.
Next rnd Knit.
Join CC and work rnds 1–8 of chart 2. Break CC, leaving 6"/15cm tail. Cont in St st with MC for approx ¾"/2cm.
Next 2 rnds K2tog to end of rnd—6 sts. Break yarn, leaving 6"/15cm tail. Weave through rem sts, pull tightly to secure.

Finishing
Block lightly to measurements. Tie I-cord into knot on top of hat. ■

Gauge
20 sts and 26 rows to 4"/10cm over St st using size 8 (5mm) needles.
Take time to check gauge.

Fair Isle Hat & Mittens

CHART 1

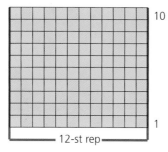

10

1

12-st rep

CHART 2

8

1

8-st rep

Color Key

Pink ice (MC)

Lime sherbert (CC)

39

Baseball Hat

Baseballs with embroidered stitching top an adorable cap—make one in your team's colors!

DESIGNED BY DEBORAH MCQUEEN CODER, AMAZING THREADS, MAPLE GROVE, MN

Size
Child's Medium

Knitted Measurements
Brim circumference (stretched)
16"/40.5cm

Materials
■ 1 3½oz/100g ball (each approx 220yd/201m) of Cascade Yarns *220 Superwash* (superwash wool) each in #814 hyacinth (A), #809 really red (B), and #817 aran (C)

■ One each sizes 3 and 6 (3.25 and 4mm) circular needle, 16"/41cm long, *or size to obtain gauge*

■ One set (5) size 6 (4mm) double-pointed needles (dpns)

■ Small amount of polyester fiberfill

■ Tapestry needle

K2, P2 Rib
(multiple of 4 sts)
Rnd 1 *K2, p2; rep from * to end of rnd.
Rep rnd 1 for k2, p2 rib.

I-Cord
*Using 2 dpns, knit one row. Without turning work, slide the sts back to the opposite end of needle to work next row from RS. Pull yarn tightly from the end of the row. Rep from * until desired length.

Gauge
20 sts and 28 rows to 4"/10cm over St st using size 6 (4mm) needles.
Take time to check gauge.

Baseball Hat

Hat

STRIPED VERSION ONLY

Note Colors should be carried up the WS between stripes.

With smaller circular needle and A, cast on 88 sts. Join to work in the rnd, being careful not to twist sts, and place marker (pm) for beg of rnd.

Work in k2, p2 rib for 1"/2.5cm, inc 2 sts evenly spaced on last rnd.

Change to larger circular needle.

*With A, knit 5 rnds.

With B, knit 5 rnds.

Rep from * once more.

SOLID VERSION ONLY

With smaller circular needle and B, cast on 88 sts. Join to work in the rnd, being careful not to twist sts, and pm for beg of rnd.

Work in k2, p2 rib for 1"/2.5cm, inc 2 sts evenly spaced on last rnd. Change to A

and knit every rnd until hat measures 4"/10cm from beg.

CROWN SHAPING

Change to dpns.

Dec rnd 1 *K8, k2tog; rep from * to end of rnd.

Next rnd Knit.

Dec rnd 2 *K7, k2tog; rep from * to end of rnd.

Next rnd Knit.

Cont to dec in this manner, knitting 1 st fewer before each dec, until 4 sts rem. Work I-cord with these 4 sts for 5"/12.5cm or desired length. Break yarn, leaving a 6"/15cm tail.

Baseball

Join C and *k1, M1; rep from * around—8 sts.

Knit 1 rnd.

Next inc rnd *K1, M1; rep from * to end of rnd—16 sts.

Knit 1 rnd.

Next inc rnd *K2, M1; rep from * to end of rnd—24 sts.

Knit 5 rnds.

Dec rnd *K1, k2tog; rep from * to end of rnd—16 sts.

Knit 1 rnd.

Next dec rnd *K2tog to end of rnd— 8 sts.

Break yarn, leaving a 6"/15cm tail.

Thread through rem sts but do not close.

Finishing

Using B, embroider the "stitching" with a running stitch as shown. Stuff baseball with fiberfill and then gather the sts to close.

Block lightly to measurements. ■

RUNNING STITCH

Colorblock Reversible Cap

Two hats for the price of one: turn it inside out and the mock cable pattern becomes a simple rib.

DESIGNED BY HEATHER BOYD, JIMMY BEANS WOOL, RENO, NV

■■□□

Size
Woman's Medium

Knitted Measurements
Brim circumference (stretched)
22"/56cm
Length 8½"/21.5cm

Materials
■ 1 3½oz/100g ball (each approx 220yd/201m) of Cascade Yarns *220 Superwash* (superwash wool) each in #900 charcoal (MC) and #893 ruby (CC)

■ Size 5 (3.75mm) circular needle, 16"/40cm long, *or size to obtain gauge*

■ One set (5) size 5 (3.75mm) double-pointed needles (dpns)

■ Stitch marker

K3, P2 Rib
(multiple of 5 sts)
Rnd 1 *K3, p2; rep from * around.
Rep rnd 1 for k3, p2 rib.

Mock Cable Pat
(multiple of 5 sts)
Rnds 1 and 2 *K3, p2; rep from * around.
Rnd 3 *Sl 1, k1, yo, k1, psso, p2; rep from * around.
Rnd 4 *K3, p2; rep from * around.
Rep rnds 1–4 for mock cable pat.

Notes
1) Change to dpns when there are too few stitches to fit comfortably on circular needle.
2) Slip all stitches purlwise.

Hat
With circular needle and CC, cast on 120 sts. Join to work in the rnd, being careful not to twist sts, and place marker (pm) for beg of rnd. Work in k3, p2 rib for 3"/7.5cm. Break CC and join MC. Starting with rnd 1, work in mock cable pat until hat measures approx 6½"/16.5 from beg, ending with rnd 4.

CROWN SHAPING
Rnd 1 *K3, p2tog, k3, p2; rep from * around—108 sts.
Rnds 2, 4, and 6 Work sts as they appear.
Rnd 3 *Sl 1, k1, yo, k1, psso, p1, sl 1, k1, yo, k1, psso, p2tog; rep from * around—96 sts.

Rnd 5 *K3, p1, k2tog, k1, p1; rep from * around—84 sts.
Rnd 7 *Sl 1, k1, yo, k1, psso, p1, sl 1, k1, psso, p1; rep from * around—72 sts.
Rnd 8 *K3, p2tog, p1; rep from * around—60 sts.
Rnd 9 *K3, p2; rep from * around.
Rnd 10 *K3, p2tog; rep from * around—48 sts.
Rnd 11 *Sl 1, k1, yo, k1, psso, p1, sl 1, k2, psso, p1; rep from * around—42 sts.
Rnd 12 *K3, p1, k2, p1; rep from * around.
Rnd 13 *K3, p1, k2tog, p1; rep from * around—36 sts.
Rnd 14 *K3, p2tog, p1; rep from * around—30 sts.
Rnd 15 *Sl 1, k2, psso, p2; rep from * around—24 sts.
Rnd 16 *K2, p2tog; rep from * around—18 sts.
Rnd 17 *K2tog, p1; rep from * around—12 sts.
Break yarn, leaving a long tail. Thread yarn through rem sts and pull tog tightly to secure.

Finishing
Block lightly to measurements. ■

Gauge
28 sts and 28 rnds to 4"/10cm over mock cable pat (unstretched) using size 5 (3.75mm) needles.
Take time to check gauge.

Felted Cable Tote

Whether you're going to the office or to the market,
a beautiful and sturdy tote is the perfect carry-all.

DESIGNED BY JULIE H. ROSE, HEAVENLY SOCKS YARNS, BELFAST, ME

■■□□

Knitted Measurements
(after felting)
Width 15"/38cm
Height 14½"/37cm
Depth 4"/10cm
Handle length 19"/48cm

Materials
■ 3 3½oz/100g hanks (each approx 220yd/201m) of Cascade Yarns *Cascade 220 Heathers* (wool) in #9490 Christmas green heather

■ Size 8 (5mm) circular needle, 32"/80cm long, *or size to obtain gauge*

■ One set (5) each sizes 6 and 8 (4 and 5mm) double-pointed needles (dpns)

■ Removable stitch markers

■ Cable needle (cn)

■ Stitch holders

■ Scrap yarn and crochet hook (for provisional cast-on)

Stitch Glossary
6-st KC (knotted cable) Sl 4 sts to cn and hold to *front*, k2, sl 2 sts back to LH needle and hold to *back*; p2 from LH needle, k2 from cn.

Provisional Cast-On
Using scrap yarn and crochet hook, ch the number of sts to cast on plus a few extra. Cut a tail and pull the tail through the last chain. With knitting needle and yarn, pick up and knit the stated number of sts through the "purl bumps" on the back of the chain. To remove waste chain, when instructed, pull out the tail from the last crochet stitch. Gently and slowly pull on the tail to unravel the crochet stitches, carefully placing each released knit stitch on a needle.

Knotted Cable Pattern
(worked in rows, over multiple of 12 sts)
Row 1 and all WS rows K3, p2, k2, p2, k3.
Rows 2, 6, and 8 P3, k2, p2, k2, p3.
Row 4 K3, 6-st KC, k3.
Rep rows 1–8 for knotted cable pat in rows.

Knotted Cable Pattern
(worked in rnds, over multiple of 12 sts)
Rnds 1–3, 5–8 P3, k2, p2, k2, p3.
Rnd 4 K3, 6-st KC, k3.
Rep rnds 1–8 for knotted cable pat in the rnd.

Note
The bag is worked from the handles down.

Gauge
18 sts and 24 rows to 4"/10cm over St st using size 8 (5mm) needles.
Take time to check gauge.

Felted Cable Tote

Tote

HANDLES (MAKE 2)

With larger dpns, cast on 12 sts using provisional cast-on. Work rows 1–8 of knotted cable pat in rows 14 times, AT THE SAME TIME, after second rep of pat work first 3 sts every row with smaller needle for a total of 12 pat reps. On final 2 reps of pat, use larger needles for all sts, ending with row 7 on final rep. Place on holder.

SIDES

*Undo provisional cast-on and place 12 handle sts on circular needle, work across in pat as est, cast on 24 sts; with RS facing, place 12 sts from opposite end of handle on LH needle and work across in pat, cast on 44 sts; rep from * with second handle—184 sts. Join to work in the rnd and place marker (pm) for beg of rnd.

Next 3 rnds Work in knotted cable pat in the rnd across all handle sts, purl rem sts. Cont as est for 12 reps of pat, ending with rnd 6 on final rep.

Next rnd Work in pat, pm 14 sts from each edge of each cable (8 markers total).

BOTTOM

Rnd 1 *P2tog tbl, purl to 2 sts before marker, p2tog; rep from * around— 16 sts dec.

Rnd 2 Purl.

Rep rnds 1 and 2 until 2 sts rem between markers on sides of bag.

Next rnd [P to one st before marker, p2tog, p2tog tbl, removing markers as necessary] twice, purl to end, removing markers. Graft rem sts tog using Kitchener st.

Finishing

Weave in ends. Felt bag by machine as foll:

1) Use a low water setting and hottest temperature in a top-loading washing machine. Add small amount of laundry detergent and jeans or towels for agitation.

2) Place item in a lingerie bag or zippered pillowcase and add to machine. Check the felting progress frequently, removing item when the individual stitches are no longer visible and item is felted to the desired size.

3) Place item in cool water to stop the felting process and remove suds. Remove from lingerie bag and roll gently in towel to remove excess water.

4) Block and shape while wet. Fold bag in at sides and bottom like a paper bag and pin into shape. Stuff with plastic bags, and allow to air dry completely. ∎

Diamond Fair Isle Hat

Two-color geometric motifs bring a modern edge to a simply shaped Fair Isle beanie.

DESIGNED BY JENN ZEYEN, THE KNITTING NEST, AUSTIN, TX

Size
Adult Medium

Knitted Measurements
Brim circumference 19"/48cm

Materials
■ 1 3½oz/100g ball (each approx 220yd/201m) of Cascade Yarns *220 Superwash* (superwash wool) each in #1975 Provence (A) and #876 sandalwood (B)

■ One pair each sizes 6 and 8 (4 and 5mm) circular needle, 16"/40cm long, *or size to obtain gauge*

■ One set (5) size 8 (5mm) double-pointed needles (dpns)

■ Stitch markers

■ Tapestry needle

Hat
With smaller circular needle and A, cast on 96 sts. Join to work in the rnd, being careful not to twist sts, and place marker (pm) for beg of rnd.
Rnd 1 *K2, p2; rep from * around.
Rnds 2–8 Rep rnd 1.
Switch to larger circular needle.
Rnd 9 Knit.
Rnd 10 *K12, pm; rep from * around.

BEG CHART 1
Rnds 1–26 *Work chart 1 over 12 sts, sl marker; rep from * to end of rnd.

Gauge
19 sts and 26 rows to 4"/10cm over St st using size 7 (4.5mm) needles.
Take time to check gauge.

119

Diamond Fair Isle Hat

CHART 1

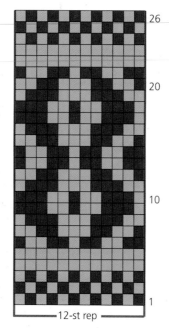

26

20

10

1

—12-st rep—

CHART 2

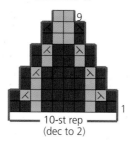

9

1

— 10-st rep —
(dec to 2)

Color and Stitch Key

- ■ Provence (A)
- ▨ Sandalwood (B)
- ◩ Ssk
- ◪ K2tog

CROWN SHAPING

Note Change to dpns when sts no longer comfortably fit on circular needle.
Rnd 1 With MC, knit around—96 sts.
Rnd 2 *K1, k2tog, k6, ssk, k1; rep from * to end of rnd—80 sts.
Rnds 3–11 Work chart 2 to end of rnd— 16 sts.
Note All decreases are made with MC.
Rnd 12 With MC, k2tog around—8 sts.

Finishing

Break yarn, leaving a 6"/15cm tail. Thread through rem sts and pull tightly to secure. Block lightly to measurements. ■

Asymmetrical Shawlette

Creative geometry turns a simple lace-edged stockinette wrap into something uniquely beautiful.

DESIGNED BY ANN SZWARC, PK YARN OVER KNIT, CLAWSON, MI

Knitted Measurements
Width at top 48"/122cm
Height at tallest point 20"/51cm

Materials
■ 2 3½oz/100g hanks (each approx 220yd/201m) of Cascade Yarns *Cascade 220 Heathers* (wool) in #9442 baby rose heather

■ Size 10 (6mm) circular needle, 32"/80cm long, *or size to obtain gauge*

■ Stitch markers

Stitch Glossary
Kfb Knit into front and back of next st— 1 st increased.

Yarn Over Bind-Off
Knit 2 sts, pass 1st st over 2nd, *yo, pass 2nd st over yo, knit next st, pass yo over st; rep from * to last st.

Shawlette
Cast on 6 sts.
Row 1 (WS) Purl.
Row 2 K2tog, yo, k1, kfb, k1, yo, k1— 8 sts.
Row 3 P1, yo, purl to end—9 sts.
Row 4 K2tog, yo, knit to last 3 sts, kfb, k1, yo, k1—11 sts.
Row 5 P1, yo, purl to end—12 sts.
Rep rows 4 and 5 until 126 sts rem.
With WS facing, rotate work clockwise until eyelets along side of the work are at top. Place marker to identify last st on needle as corner st. [Pick up and k 1 st, yo] in each eyelet across side, then pick

Gauge
17 sts and 21 rows to 4"/10cm over St st using size 10 (6mm) needles.
Take time to check gauge.

Asymmetrical Shawlette

up and k 1 st in cast-on row—207 sts. Work two set-up rows as foll:
Row 1 Knit to marker, sl marker, k1, *k1, yo, k2tog, yo; rep from * to last 2 sts, k2tog—247 sts.
Row 2 Purl.

LACE EDGING
Row 1 (RS) K1, yo, k2tog, *yo, k1, k2tog; rep from * to marker, yo, sl marker, k1 (corner stitch), yo, *ssk, k1, yo; rep from * to last 3 sts, ssk, yo, k1—249 sts.
Row 2 and all WS rows Purl.
Row 3 K1, yo, k2tog, yo, *k1, k2tog, yo; rep from * to 1 st before marker, kfb, sl marker, k1 (corner stitch), kfb, *yo, ssk, k1; rep from * to last 3 sts, yo, ssk, yo, k1—253 sts.
Row 5 K1, yo, k2tog, yo, k1, *k2tog, yo, k1; rep from * to 2 sts before marker, yo, k2tog, yo, sl marker, k1 (corner stitch), yo, ssk, yo, *k1, yo, ssk; rep from * to last 4 sts, k1, yo, ssk, yo, k1—257 sts.
Row 7 K1, yo, *k2tog, yo, k1; rep from * to 4 sts before marker, k2tog, [k1, yo] twice, sl marker, k1, [yo, k1] twice, ssk, *k1, yo, ssk; rep from * to last st, yo, k1—261 sts.
Row 9 K1, yo, *k2tog, yo, k1; rep from * to 6 sts before marker, k2tog, yo, k2tog, [k1, yo] twice, sl marker, k1, [yo, k1] twice, ssk, yo, ssk, *k1, yo, ssk; rep from * to last st, yo, k1—265 sts.
Bind off using yarn over bind-off.

Finishing
Block lightly to measurements. ▪

Felted Bowls

Keep your knitting notions or other knickknacks stored in style with these pretty ruffled bowls.

DESIGNED BY BECKY CURRAN, REDLANDS YARN COMPANY, REDLANDS, CA

Sizes
Instructions are written for Small bowl. Changes for Medium and Large bowls are in parentheses.

Knitted Measurements
(after felting)
Height 3½ (4.5, 5.5)"/9 (11.5, 14)cm
Circumference at widest point 14 (17, 20)"/35.5 (43, 51)cm

Materials
■ 1 3½oz/100g hank (each approx 220yd/201m) of Cascade Yarns *Cascade 220* (wool) each in #8400 charcoal (A), #8401 silver grey (B), and #8011 Aspen heather (C)

■ Size 9 (5.5mm) circular needle, 16"/41cm long, *or size to obtain gauge*

■ One set (4) size 9 (5.5mm) double-pointed needles (dpns)

■ Small glass jar that will fit into the interior of your bowl(s)

■ Stitch markers

Bowls
With circular needle and A (B, C), cast on 70 (90, 110) sts.
Join to work in the rnd, being careful not to twist sts. Place marker (pm) for beg of rnd.

Gauge
16 sts and 20 rows to 4"/10cm over St st using size 9 (5.5mm) needles.
Take time to check gauge.

Felted Bowls

RUFFLE

Work 3 (5, 7) rnds in garter st (purl 1 rnd, knit 1 rnd), beg with a purl rnd.

Dec rnd *K2, pass 1st st over 2nd st and off needle; rep from * to end of rnd—35 (45, 55) sts.

Rnd 1 *K 5 (7, 9), k2tog; rep from * to end of rnd—30 (40, 50) sts.

Rnds 2–9 Knit.

Rnd 10 *K 3 (4, 5), M1; rep from * to end of rnd—40 (50, 60) sts.

Rnd 11 Knit.

Rnd 12 *K 4 (5, 6), M1; rep from * to end of rnd—50 (60, 70) sts.

Rnd 13 Knit.

Rnd 14 *K 5 (6, 7), M1; rep from * to end of rnd—60 (70, 80) sts.

Rnd 15 Knit.

Rnd 16 *K 6 (7, 8), M1; rep from * to end of rnd—70 (80, 90) sts.

Rnd 17 Knit.

MEDIUM AND LARGE BOWLS ONLY

Rnd 18 *Knit (8, 9), M1; rep from * to end of rnd—(90, 100) sts.

LARGE BOWL ONLY

Rnd 19 Knit.

Rnd 20 *K10, M1; rep from * to end of rnd—110 sts.

ALL SIZES

Knit 20 (26, 32) rnds.

BASE DECREASES

Note For Large, beg with rnd 1, for Medium, beg with rnd 5, for Small, beg with rnd 9.

Rnd 1 *K9, k2tog; rep from * to end of rnd—100 sts.

Rnd 2 and all even-numbered rnds Knit.

Rnd 3 *K8, k2tog; rep from * to end of rnd—90 sts.

Rnd 5 *K7, k2tog; rep from * to end of rnd—80 sts.

Rnd 7 *K6, k2tog; rep from * to end of rnd—70 sts.

Rnd 9 *K5, k2tog; rep from * to end of rnd—60 sts.

Rnd 11 *K4, k2tog; rep from * to end of rnd—50 sts.

Rnd 13 *K3, k2tog; rep from * to end of rnd—40 sts.

Rnd 15 *K2, k2tog; rep from * to end of rnd—30 sts.

Rnd 17 *K1, k2tog; rep from * to end of rnd—20 sts.

Rnd 19 K2tog to end of rnd—10 sts.

Finishing

Break yarn, leaving 12"/30cm tail. Thread through rem sts and pull tightly to secure. Weave in all ends.

MACHINE FELTING

1) Use a low water setting and hottest temperature in a top-loading washing machine. Add small amount of laundry detergent and jeans or towels for agitation.

2) Place item in a lingerie bag or zippered pillowcase and add to machine. Check the felting progress frequently, removing item when the individual stitches are no longer visible and item is felted to the desired size.

3) Place item in cool water to stop the felting process and remove suds. Remove from lingerie bag and roll gently in towel to remove excess water.

4) Block and shape while wet. Pin into shape or stuff with plastic bags, and allow to air dry completely. ∎

Two-Color Cable Cap

This striking hat is a showcase of design, with single-row stripes, colorful cables, and a brim knit in two layers to provide structure.

DESIGNED BY MARIN J. MELCHIOR, CACKLIN' HENS, MIDDLEBURY, VT

Size
Woman's Small/Medium

Knitted Measurements
Brim circumference (slightly stretched) 22"/56cm
Diameter at widest point 10"/25.5cm

Materials
■ 1 3½oz/100g hank (each approx 220yd/201m) of Cascade Yarns *Cascade 220* (wool) each in #4002 jet (A) and #9404 ruby (B)

■ One each sizes 4 and 6 (3.5 and 4mm) circular needle, 16"/41cm long, *or size to obtain gauge*

■ One set (5) size 6 (4mm) double-pointed needles (dpns)

■ Cable needle (cn)

Notes
1) Yarn should always be carried across behind cables.
2) At the beginning of each row, wrap and twist colors to secure and provide an even color transition.

Stitch Glossary
8-st LSC Sl 4 sts to cn and hold to *front*, sl 4 sts in B to RH needle, [k2, yo, k2] from cn.
Pdec P2tog, p until 2 sts before cable, p2tog tbl.

K2, P2 Rib
(multiple of 4 sts)
Rnd 1 *K2, p2; rep from * to end of rnd.
Rep rnd 1 for k2, p2 rib.

Cap
Using smaller needles and A, cast on 108 sts. Join to work in the rnd, being careful not to twist sts, and place marker (pm) for beg of rnd.
Work in k2, p2 rib for 1½"/4cm.

Inc rnd *K1, M1, k1, p1, M1, p1; rep from * around—162 sts.
Change to larger circular needle.
Rnd 1 With A, p9, M1 p-st, [k2, yo, k2, sl 4, p9, M1, p10] 5 times, k2, yo, k2, sl 4, p10—168 sts.
Rnd 2 Join B, p10, [sl 2, drop yo, sl 2, k2, yo, k2, p20] 5 times, sl 2, drop yo, sl 2, k2, yo, k2, p10.
Rnd 3 With A, p10, [k2, yo, k2, sl 2, drop yo, sl 2, p20] 5 times, k2, yo, k2, sl 2, drop yo, sl 2, p10.
Rnds 4 and 5 Rep rnds 2 and 3.
Rnd 6 Rep rnd 2.
Rnd 7 With A, p10, [8-st LSC, p20] 5 times, 8-st LSC, p10.
Rnd 8 With B, p10, [sl 2, drop yo, sl 2, k2, yo, k2, p20] 5 times, sl 2, drop yo, sl 2, k2, yo, k2, p10.
Rnd 9 With A, p10, [k2, yo, k2, sl 2, drop yo, sl 2, p20] 5 times, k2, yo, k2, sl 2, drop yo, sl 2, p10.

Gauges
22 sts and 28 rnds to 4"/10cm over St st using size 6 (4mm) needles.
20 sts and 32 rnds to 4"/10cm over cable pat using size 6 (4mm) needles.
Take time to check gauges.

Two-Color Cable Cap

Rnds 10–13 Work rnds 8 and 9 twice more.
Rnd 14 With B, p10, [4-st LSC, p14] 5 times, 4-st LSC, p10.
Rep rnds 1–14 once more.

CROWN SHAPING
Rnd 1 With A, purl to cable, [sl 2, drop yo, sl 2, k2, yo, k2, purl to cable] 5 times, sl 2, drop yo, sl2, k2, yo, k2, purl to end.
Rnd 2 With B, purl to 2 sts before cable, p2tog tbl, [k2, yo, k2, sl 2, drop yo, sl 2, pdec] 5 times, k2, yo, k2, sl 2, drop yo, sl 2, p2tog, p to end.
Rnds 3–6 Rep rnds 1 and 2 twice more.
Rnd 7 With A, purl to cable [8-st LSC, p20] 5 times, 8-st LSC, purl to end.

Rnd 8 With B, purl to 2 sts before cable, p2tog tbl [k4, sl 4, pdec] 5 times, k4, sl 4, p2tog, purl to end.
Rnd 9 With A, purl to cable, [sl 4, k4, purl to cable] 5 times, sl 4, k4, p to end.
Rnds 10–15 Rep rnds 8 and 9 three times more.
Rnd 16 With B, purl to 2 sts before cable, p2tog tbl, [sl 4 to cn and hold in *front*, sl 4 in B onto LH needle, k4 from cn, purl to cable] 5 times, sl 4 to cn and hold in *front*, sl 4 in B onto LH needle, k4 from cn, p2tog, p to end.
Rnd 17 With A, p3; [with A, k4; with B, k4; with A, p6] 5 times; with A, k4; with B, k4; with A, p3.
Rnd 18 With B, p1; with B, p2tog tbl; [with A, k4; with B, k4; pdec] 5 times; with A, k4; with B, k4; with B, p1; with B, p2tog.
Rnd 19 With A, p2; [with A, k4; with B, k4; with A, p4] 5 times; with A, k4; with B, k4; with A, p2.
Move marker one st to the right.
Rnd 20 With B, p2tog tbl; [with A, k4; with B, k4; pdec] 5 times; with A, k4; with B, k4; with B, p2tog.
Rnd 21 *With A, p2tog; with A, k3; with B, k3; with B, p2tog; rep from * to end of rnd.
Rnd 22 With B, purl to 2 sts before cable, p2tog tbl [sl 4 to cn and hold in *front*, sl 4 in B onto LH needle, k4 from cn, purl to cable] 5 times, sl 4 to cn and hold in *front*, sl 4 in B onto LH needle, k4 from cn, p2tog, purl to end.
Rnd 23 *With B, ssk, k2; with A, k2, k2tog; rep from * to end of rnd.
Rnd 24 *With B, ssk, k1; with A, k1, k2tog; rep from * to end of rnd.
Rnd 25 *With b, ssk; with A, k2tog; rep from * to end of rnd—12 sts.
Break yarns, leaving a 6"/15cm tail, draw both yarns through rem sts and pull tightly to secure.

Brim
With B, pick up and k 21 sts along bottom edge of hat (decide where you want center of hat to be, pick up 10 sts on either side of that point plus 1 st at that point).
Rnd 1 (WS) Purl.
Rnd 2 (RS) K2, M1, pm, k16, pm, M1, k2, pick up and k 2 sts along hat edge.
Rnd 3 (WS) Purl, pick up and k 2 sts along hat edge.
Rnd 4 (RS) Knit to 1st marker, M1, sl marker, k16, sl marker, M1, knit to end, pick up and k 2 sts along hat edge.
Rnd 5 (WS) Purl to end, pick up and k 2 sts along hat edge.
Rep rnds 4 and 5 nine times more.
Next (turning) rnd (RS) With A, purl.
Rnd 1 (WS) Sl 2, psso, bind off 1, purl to end.
Rnd 2 (RS) Sl 2, psso, bind off 1, knit until 2 sts before marker, ssk, k16, k2tog, knit to end.
Rep these two rnds until 20 sts rem, end with RS rnd.

Finishing
Sew brim. Block around a 10"/25.5cm plate. ∎

Colorblock Pullover

A bright blend of solids and heathers livens up a stockinette baby sweater with rolled edges.

DESIGNED BY SUDHA SARIN, NINE RUBIES KNITTING, SAN MATEO, CA

■■□□

Sizes
Instructions are written for size 6 months. Changes for sizes 12, 18, and 24 months are in parentheses.

Knitted Measurements
Chest circumference 19 (20½, 21½, 22½)"/48.5 (52, 54.5, 57)cm
Length 11 (12, 12¾, 14)"/28 (30.5, 32.5, 35.5)cm
Upper arm circumference 8 (9, 9½, 10)"/20.5 (23, 24, 25.5)cm

Materials
■ 1 3½oz/100g ball (each approx 220yd/201m) of Cascade Yarns *220 Superwash* (superwash wool) each in #1925 cobalt heather (MC) and #906 chartreuse (A)

■ 1 3½oz/100g ball (each approx 220yd/201m) of Cascade Yarns *220 Superwash Quatros* (superwash wool) in #1957 antiqua (B)

■ One pair size 6 (4mm) needles *or size to obtain gauge*

■ Size 6 (4mm) circular needle, 16"/40cm long
■ Stitch marker
■ Stitch holders

K1, P1 Rib
(over an even number of sts)
Row 1 (RS) *K1 p1; rep from * to end.
Row 2 *P1, k1; rep from * to end.
Rep rows 1 and 2 for k1, p1 rib.

Back
With straight needles and MC, cast on 53 (56, 59, 62) sts. Beg with a purl (WS) row, work 29 (31, 33, 35) rows in St st, end with a WS row.
Break MC and join B. With B, work even in St st for a further 24 (26, 28, 30) rows, end with a WS row.
Break B and join A. With A, work even in St st for a further 24 (26, 28, 30) rows, end with a WS row.

SHAPE SHOULDERS
Bind off 6 (7, 7, 8) sts at beg of next 2 rows and 6 (6, 7, 7) sts at beg of next 2 rows—29 (30, 31, 32) sts. Leave rem sts on holder for back neck.

Front
Work as for back until 10 (12, 12, 14) rows have been worked with A, ending with a WS row.

SHAPE NECK
Next row (RS) K19 (20, 21, 22), turn, work on these sts only.
Purl 1 row.
Cont in St st as est, dec 1 st at neck edge every row 5 times, then every RS row twice, ending with a RS row—12 (13, 14, 15) sts.
Work 3 (3, 5, 5) rows even, ending with a WS row.

SHAPE SHOULDERS
Bind off 6 (7, 7, 8) sts at beg of next row—6 (6, 7, 7) sts. Work 1 row even.
Bind off.
With RS facing, return to sts on hold, rejoin A, k15 (16, 17, 18) and slip these sts to holder for center front neck, k to end of row—19 (20, 21, 22) sts. Work second half of neck as for first, reversing shaping.

Gauge
22 sts and 28 rows to 4"/10cm over St st using size 6 (4mm) needles.
Take time to check gauge.

Colorblock Pullover

Sleeves

With B, cast on 28 (28, 32, 32) sts. Work 3 rows in k1, p1 rib, ending with a WS row. Break B and join MC.
Starting with a knit (RS) row, work in St st, inc 1 st at each end of 5th and every following 4th row 7 (9, 9, 10) times—44 (48, 52, 54) sts. Work even until piece measures 6½ (7, 7½, 8)"/16.5 (18, 19, 20.5)cm from beg, ending with a WS row. Bind off.

Finishing

Block pieces to measurements. Sew shoulder seams.

NECKBAND

With circular needle and A, pick up and k 70 (72, 74, 76) sts evenly around neck opening, including sts on holders. Join to work in the rnd and place marker (pm) for beg of rnd. Work 10 rnds in St st (k every rnd). Bind off loosely.

Pm 4 (4½, 4¾, 5)"/10 (11.5, 12, 12.5)cm down from shoulder seam on front and back for armholes. With center of bound-off edge of sleeve at shoulder seam, sew top of sleeve between markers. Sew side and sleeve seams. Block lightly to measurements. ■

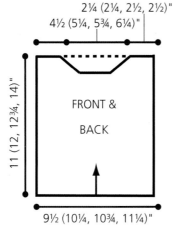

2¼ (2¼, 2½, 2½)"
4½ (5¼, 5¾, 6¼)"

FRONT &
BACK

11 (12, 12¾, 14)"

9½ (10¼, 10¾, 11¼)"

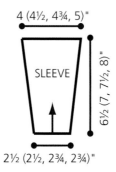

4 (4½, 4¾, 5)"

SLEEVE

6½ (7, 7½, 8)"

2½ (2½, 2¾, 2¾)"

Rainbow Scales Wrap

Stripes are set off with slipped stitches, creating a lovely tiled look edged with a single ruffle.

DESIGNED BY RACHEL KEENER, OLD SPINNING WHEEL YARN SHOP, KILLEEN, TX

Knitted Measurements
Height 14"/35.5cm
Length 39½"/100cm

Materials
■ 2 3½oz/100g hanks (each approx 220yd/201m) of Cascade Yarns *Cascade 220 Heathers* (wool) in #2423 Montmarte (A)

■ 1 hank each in #9449 midnight heather (B), #2433 Pacific (C), #9345 wisteria (D), and #9322 silver spruce heather (E)

■ One pair size 8 (5mm) needles *or size to obtain gauge*

■ One 2"/5cm button

Stitch Glossary
RT Knit 2nd st on LH needle, leaving it on LH needle, knit 1st st, sl both sts tog to RH needle.

LT Knit 2nd st on LH needle tbl, leaving it on LH needle, knit 1st st tbl, sl both sts tog to RH needle.

Kfb Knit into front and back of next st— 1 st increased.

Gauges
17 sts and 23 rows to 4"/10cm over St st using size 8 (5mm) needles.
18 sts and 26 rows to 4"/10cm over stripe pat using size 8 (5mm) needles.
Take time to check gauges.

Rainbow Scales Wrap

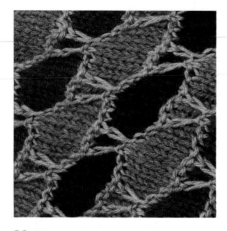

Notes
1) Sl all sts purlwise (sl sts wyib on RS rows and sl sts wyif on WS rows).
2) Twist yarn at back of work where border and stripe colors meet to prevent gaps in work.

Wrap
With A, cast on 68 sts.
Knit 4 rows.

BEG STRIPE PAT
Row 1 (RS) With A, k4; with B, k4, sl 2 wyib, [k8, sl 2 wyib] 5 times, k4; with A, k4.
Row 2 (WS) With A, k4; with B, p4, sl 2 wyif, [p8, sl 3 wyif] 5 times, p4; with A, k4.
Rows 3–6 Rep rows 1 and 2 twice.
Row 7 With A, k7, RT, LT, [k6, RT, LT] 5 times, k8.
Row 8 With A, knit.
Row 9 With A, k4, sl 1; with C, [k8, sl 2] 5 times, k8; with A, sl 1, k4.
Row 10 With A, k4, sl 1; with C, [p8, sl 2] 5 times, p8; with A, sl 1, k4.
Rows 11–14 Rep rows 1 and 2 twice.
Row 15 With A, k4, LT, [k6, RT, LT] 4 times, RT, k4.

Row 16 With A, knit.
Row 17 With A, k4; with D, k4, sl 2 wyib, [k8, sl 2 wyib] 5 times, k4; with A, k4.
Row 18 (WS) With A, k4; with D, p4, sl 2 wyif, [p8, sl 3 wyif] 5 times, p4; with A, k4.
Rows 19–22 Rep rows 17 and 18 twice.
Row 23 With A, k7, RT, LT, [k6, RT, LT] 5 times, k8.
Row 24 With A, knit.
Row 25 With A, k4, sl 1; with E, [k8, sl 2] 5 times, k8; with A, sl 1, k4.
Row 26 With A, k4, sl 1; with E, [p8, sl 2] 5 times, p8; with A, sl 1, k4.
Rows 27–30 Rep rows 25 and 26 twice.
Row 31 With A, k4, LT, [k6, RT, LT] 4 times, RT, k4.
Row 32 With A, knit.
Rep rows 1–32 six times more, then rows 1–24 once.
With A, knit 2 rows.
Dec row 1 K3tog across.
Knit 1 row.
Dec row 2 *K2tog, k2; rep from * to end.
Knit 11 rows.

BUTTONHOLE
Row 1 K6, bind off 5 sts, k6.
Row 2 K6, cast on 5 sts, k6.
Knit 10 rows and bind off.

RUFFLE
Pick up and knit 68 sts at the cast-on edge.
Row 1 Kfb to end.
Row 2 Knit.
Rep rows 1 and 2 until ruffle measures desired width.
Bind off.

Finishing
Block lightly to measurements. Sew on button approx 2"/5cm from top edge, just inside ruffle. ∎

Scalloped Lace Capelet

A delicate lacy capelet with scalloped edges gets extra visual interest from a subtly variegated yarn.

DESIGNED BY EDIE NELSON, ARTISANS' CO-OP, BODEGA, CA

Knitted Measurements
Circumference 26"/66cm
Height 9"/23cm

Materials
- 1 3½oz/100g ball (each approx 220yd/201m) of Cascade Yarns *220 Superwash Paints* (superwash wool) in #9874 Arctic ice
- Size 9 (5.5mm) circular needle, 24"/60cm long, *or size to obtain gauge*
- Stitch markers

Stitch Glossary
M1R Insert LH needle from back to front under the strand between last st worked and next st on LH needle. K into the front loop to twist the st.
M1L Insert LH needle from front to back under the strand between last st worked and next st on LH needle. K into the back loop to twist the st.

Scallop Lace Pattern
(multiple of 10 sts)
Rnd 1 Knit.
Rnd 2 *Yo, k3, SK2P, k3, yo, k1; rep from * to end of rnd.
Rnd 3 Knit.
Rnd 4 *K1, yo, k2, SK2P, k2, yo, k1, p1; rep from * to end of rnd.
Rnd 5 *K9, p1; rep from * to end of rnd.
Rnd 6 *K2, yo, k1, SK2P, k1, yo, k2, p1; rep from * to end of rnd.
Rnd 7 *K9, p1; rep from * to end of rnd.
Rnd 8 *K3, yo, SK2P, yo, k3, p1; rep from * to end of rnd.
Rep rnds 1–8 for scallop lace pat.

Note
For ease, place marker after each repeat of the scallop lace pattern—13 repeats total.

Capelet
Cast on 130 stitches. Join to work in the round, being careful not to twist, and place marker for beg of rnd.
Work rnds 1–8 of scallop lace pat 5 times.

RUFFLE
Rnd 1 and all odd-numbered rnds Knit.
Rnd 2 K1, *M1L, k4, M1R, k3; rep from * to last 2 sts, k2.
Rnd 4 K2, *M1L, k4, M1R, k5; rep from * to last 3 sts, k3.
Rnd 6 K3, *M1L, k4, M1R, k7; rep from * to last 4 sts, k4.
Rnd 8 K4, *M1L, k4, M1R, k9; rep from * to last 5 sts, k5.
Bind off loosely.

Finishing
Block lightly to measurements. ∎

Gauge
16 sts and 20 rows to 4"/10cm over St st using size 9 (5.5mm) needles.
Take time to check gauge.

Beaded Ruffle Shawlette

Beads incorporated into each ruffle at the edge add a touch of glamour to a sweet little shawl.

DESIGNED BY SHARON E. MOONEY, HANDS ON KNITTING CENTER, REDLANDS, CA

Knitted Measurements
Width at top edge 48"/122cm
Height at center 9"/23cm

Materials
■ 2 3½oz/100g balls (each approx 220yd/201m) of Cascade Yarns *220 Superwash Paints* (superwash wool) in #9647 pink hydrangeas

■ Size 7 (4.5mm) circular needle, 40"/102cm long, *or size to obtain gauge*

■ Stitch markers, including removable markers

■ 288 size 6/0 glass beads (Miyuki 533 Dyed Salmon Silver Lined Alabaster used in sample)

■ Size 13/14 (.9mm) steel crochet hook, or size to fit through beads

Stitch Glossary
Hb (hook bead) Place bead onto crochet hook, draw next st from LH needle through bead using hook. Sl st to RH needle without working.

Short Row Wrap and Turn (w&t)
On RS row (on WS row)
1) Wyib (wyif), sl next st purlwise.
2) Move yarn between the needles to the front (back).
3) Sl the same st back to LH needle. Turn work. One st is wrapped.
4) When working the wrapped st, insert RH needle under the wrap and work it tog with the corresponding st on needle.

Shawlette
Cast on 738 sts.
Row 1 (RS) K2, place marker (pm), *k23, (pm); rep from * to last 23 sts, k23.
Row 2 (WS) Knit.
Row 3 P2, *sl m, ssk, k8, hb, k8, k2tog, p2; rep from * to end—674 sts, 21 sts bet markers.
Row 4 *K2, p19, sl marker; rep to last 2 sts, k2.
Row 5 P2, *sl m, ssk, k7, hb, k7, k2tog, p2; rep from * to end—610 sts, 19 sts bet markers.
Row 6 *K2, p17, sl m; rep from * to last 2 sts, k2.
Row 7 P2, *sl m, ssk, k6, hb, k6, k2tog, p2; rep from * to end—546 sts, 17 sts bet markers.
Row 8 *K2, p15, sl m; rep from * to last 2 sts, k2.
Row 9 P2, *sl m, ssk, k5, hb, k5, k2tog, p2; rep from * to end—482 sts, 15 sts bet markers.
Row 10 *K2, p13, sl m; rep from * to last 2 sts, k2.
Row 11 P2, *sl m, ssk, k4, hb, k4, k2tog, p2; rep from * to end—418 sts, 13 sts bet markers.
Row 12 *K2, p11, sl m; rep from * to last 2 sts, k2.
Row 13 P2, *sl m, ssk, k3, hb, k3, k2tog, p2; rep from * to end—354 sts, 11 sts bet markers.
Row 14 *K2, p9, sl m; rep from * to last 2 sts, k2.
Row 15 P2, *sl m, ssk, k2, hb, k2, k2tog, p2; rep from * to end—290 sts, 9 sts bet markers.
Row 16 *K2, p7, sl m; rep from * to last 2 sts, k2.
Row 17 P2, *sl m, ssk, k1, hb, k1, k2tog, p2; rep from * to end—226 sts, 7 sts bet markers.

Gauge
20 sts and 28 rows to 4"/10cm over St st using size 7 (4.5mm) needles.
Take time to check gauge.

Beaded Ruffle Shawlette

Row 18 *K2, p5, sl m; rep from * to last 2 sts, k2.

Row 19 P2, *sl m, ssk, hb, k2tog, p2; rep from * to end—162 sts, 5 sts bet markers.

Row 20 *K2, p3, remove marker; rep from * to last 2 sts, k2.

Row 21 *P2, k3; rep from * to last 2 sts, p2.

From now on you will use only removable markers.

Row 22 K to end. Do not turn; pick up and p 18 sts evenly along adjoining side of ruffle—180 sts. Turn.

Row 23 K to end, do not turn, pick up and k 18 sts evenly along adjoining side of ruffle—198 sts. Turn.

Row 24 P124, w&t, pm through newly wrapped st.

Row 25 K50, w&t, pm through newly wrapped st (center 50 sts are now "framed" by markers).

Row 26 P to marker, remove marker, p wrapped st tog with its wrap, p5, w&t, pm through newly wrapped st.

Row 27 K to marker, remove marker, k wrapped st tog with its wrap, k5, w&t, pm through newly wrapped st.

Rep rows 26 and 27 until all sts are worked; last 2 rows will end with p7 (WS), and k7 (RS).

TOP BORDER
Rows 1–3 Knit.
Bind off all sts.

Finishing
Block lightly to measurements. ■

Cabled Paperbag Hat

Cables meet at the top in a cute and cozy cap with a drawstring tie for a perfect fit.

DESIGNED BY VICTORIA WICKHAM, HEARTLAND FIBER CO., WINTERSET, IA

Size
Woman's Small

Knitted Measurements
Brim circumference (stretches to fit)
16"/40cm
Height (with brim folded) 9"/ 23cm

Materials
■ 2 3½oz/100g hanks (each approx 220yd/106m) of Cascade Yarns *Cascade 220* (wool) in #9484 stratosphere
■ One each sizes 6 and 8 (4 and 5mm) circular needle, 16"/40cm long, *or size to obtain gauge*
■ One set (5) size 8 (5mm) double-pointed needles (dpns)
■ Size H/8 (5mm) crochet hook
■ Cable needle (cn)
■ Stitch markers

Stitch Glossary
RT Sl 1 st to cn and hold to *back*, k1, k1 from cn.
3-st RC Sl 1 st to cn and hold to *back,* k2, k1 from cn.
3-st LC Sl 2 sts to cn and hold to *front*, k1, k2 from cn.
3-st RPC Sl 1 st to cn and hold to *back*, k2, p1 from cn.
3-st LPC Sl 2 sts to cn and hold to *front*, p1, k2 from cn.
5-st RPC Sl 3 sts to cn and hold to *back*, k2, slip last st from cn, p1, k2 from cn.

Gauge
17 sts and 25 rows to 4"/10cm over St st using size 8 (5mm) needles.
Take time to check gauge.

50 Cabled Paperbag Hat

K1, P1 Rib
(multiple of 2 sts)
Rnd 1 *K1, p1; rep from * to end of rnd.
Rep rnd 1 for k1, p1 rib.

Cable Pattern
(multiple of 19 sts)
Rnd 1 (RS) *P5, 3-st RC, p1, 3-st LC, p5, RT; rep from * around.
Rnd 2 *P5, k3, p1, k3, p5, k2; rep from * around.
Rnd 3 *P4, 3-st RC, p1, k1, p1, 3-st LC, p4, RT; rep from * around.
Rnd 4 *P4, k3, p1, k1, p1, k3, p4, k2; rep from * around.
Rnd 5 *P3, 3-st RC, p1, [k1, p1] twice, 3-st LC, p3, RT; rep from * around.
Rnd 6 *P3, k3, p1, [k1, p1] twice, k3, p3, k2; rep from * around.
Rnd 7 *P2, 3-st RC, p1, [k1, p1] 3 times, 3-st LC, p2, RT; rep from * around.
Rnd 8 *P2, k3, p1, [k1, p1] 3 times, k3, p2, k2; rep from * around.
Rnd 9 *P2, k2, p1, [k1, p1] 4 times, k2, p2, RT; rep from * around.
Rnd 10 *P2, k2, p1, [k1, p1] 4 times, k2, p2, k2; rep from * around.
Rnd 11 *P2, 3-st LPC, p1, [k1, p1] 3 times, 3-st RPC, p2, RT; rep from * around.
Rnd 12 *P3, k2, p1 [k1, p1] 3 times, k2, p3, k2; rep from * around.
Rnd 13 *P3, 3-st LPC, p1, [k1, p1] twice, 3-st RPC, p3, RT; rep from * around.
Rnd 14 *P4, k2, p1, [k1, p1] twice, k2, p4, k2; rep from * around.
Rnd 15 *P4, 3-st LPC, p1, k1, p1, 3-st RPC, p4, RT; rep from * around.
Rnd 16 *P5, k2, p1, k1, p1, k2, p5, k2; rep from * around.
Rnd 17 *P5, 3-st LPC, p1, 3-st RPC, p5, RT; rep from * around.
Rnd 18 *P6, k2, p1, k2, p6, k2; rep from * around.
Rnd 19 *P6, 5-st RPC, p6, RT; rep from * around.
Rnd 20 *P6, k5, p6, k2; rep from * around.
Rep rnds 1–20 for cable pat.

Hat
With smaller needle, cast on 100 sts. Join, being careful not to twist sts, and place marker for beg of rnd.
Work in k1, p1 rib until piece measures approx 6"/15cm. Work one more rnd, inc 14 sts evenly around—114 sts.
Change to larger needle and beg cable pat. Work even in pat until piece measures approx 5½"/14cm from beg of cable pat, ending with rnd 15.

CROWN SHAPING
Note Change to dpns when sts no longer comfortably fit on circular needle.
Next rnd *P1, p2tog, p1, [k2tog] twice, p1, [k2tog] twice, p1, p2tog, p1, k2tog; rep from * around—72 sts.
Next rnd *K4, k2tog, yo; rep from * around.
Work in k1, p1 rib for 1½"/4cm. Bind off loosely in pat.

Finishing
Block lightly to measurements.
With yarn held double, crochet a chain approx 22"/56cm long. Fasten off and trim ends. Thread through yarn overs, starting at center front, and tie in a bow at the front. ■

Cabled Fingerless Mitts

Simple cables and a hole left for the thumb add up to an easy but eye-catching pair of mitts.

DESIGNED BY SUNNI SCRIVNER, YARN, EUREKA, CA

Size
Woman's Small/Medium

Knitted Measurements
Circumference (unstretched) 7"/18cm
Length 7"/18cm

Materials
■ 1 3½oz/100g hank (each approx 220yd/201m) of Cascade Yarns *Cascade 220* (wool) in #9076 mint
■ One pair size 7 (4.5mm) needles *or size to obtain gauge*
■ Cable needle (cn)

Stitch Glossary
4-st LC Sl 2 sts to cn and hold to *front*; k2, k2 from cn.
4-st RC Sl 2 sts to cn and hold to *back*; k2, k2 from cn.

Cable Pattern A
(worked over 32 sts)
Row 1 (RS) P2, [k4, p2] 5 times.
Row 2 [K2, p4] 5 times, k2.
Row 3 P2, [4-st LC, p2] 5 times.
Row 4 [K2, p4] 5 times, k2.
Rep rows 1–4 for cable pat A.

Cable Pattern B
(worked over 32 sts)
Row 1 (RS) P2, [k4, p2] 5 times.
Row 2 [K2, p4] 5 times, k2.
Row 3 P2, [4-st RC, p2] 5 times.
Row 4 [K2, p4] 5 times, k2.
Rep rows 1–4 for cable pat B.

Notes
1) Mitts are worked flat and then seamed, leaving a hole for the thumb.
2) Slip stitches purlwise at beginning of every row.

Right Mitt
Cast on 42 sts.

Row 1 (RS) Sl 1, k1, [p1, k1] twice, work row 1 of cable pat A over next 32 sts, k1, p1, k1, k1 tbl.
Row 2 Sl 1, p1, k1, p1, work row 2 of cable pat A over next 32 sts, [p1, k1] twice, p1, k1 tbl.
Cont as est, working appropriate row of cable pat A, until piece measures approx 7"/18cm from beg, end with row 4 of pat. Bind off in pat.

Left Mitt
Cast on 42 sts.
Row 1 (RS) Sl 1, k1, p1, k1, work row 1 of cable pat B over next 32 sts, [k1, p1] twice, k1, k1 tbl.
Row 2 Sl 1, p1, [k1, p1] twice, work row 2 of cable pat B over next 32 sts, p1, k1, p1, k1 tbl.
Cont as est, working appropriate row of cable pat B, until piece measures approx 7"/18cm from beg, end with row 4 of pat. Bind off in pat.

Finishing
Starting at bound-off edge, sew side edges tog for 1½"/4cm. Starting at cast-on edge, sew side edges tog for 3¾"/9.5cm. Leave rem space open for thumb.
Block lightly to measurements. ■

Gauge
24 sts and 28 rnds to 4"/10cm over cable pat using size 7 (4.5mm) needles.
Take time to check gauge.

Felted Elephant

Big, floppy ears and a playfully curvy trunk lend personality to a cuddly companion.

DESIGNED BY THE DOLLY-MAMAS, ELISSA'S CREATIVE WAREHOUSE, NEEDHAM, MA

Knitted Measurements
Height (after felting) Approx 8"/20cm

Materials
- 1 3½oz/100g hank (each approx 220yd/201m) of Cascade Yarns *Cascade 220 Heathers* (wool) in #2449 peony pink
- One pair size 9 (5.5mm) needles *or size to obtain gauge*
- Stitch markers
- Polyester fiberfill
- Wool roving and felting needle (for eyes)
- Non-felting scrap yarn (cotton, silk, etc.)

Stitch Glossary
Kfb Knit into front and back of next st—1 st increased.

Elephant
LEGS
Cast on 24 sts.
Rows 1–16 Beg with a knit (RS) row, work in St st.
Break yarn, leaving a 6"/15cm tail. Leave sts on needle. Cast on 24 sts and rep rows 1–16 (2 legs on needle; 48 sts total).

BODY
Row 17 (RS) Knit.
Rows 18 and 19 Work in St st.
Row 20 P14, place marker (pm), p20, pm, p14.
Row 21 Knit to 2 sts before marker, k2tog, sl marker, knit to marker, sl marker, k2tog tbl, knit to end—46 sts.
Rows 22–24 Work in St st.
Rep last 4 rows three more times—40 sts.
Rows 36–50 Work in St st, remove markers.

HEAD
Row 51 [K2tog] across—20 sts.
Row 52 [Kfb] across—40 sts.
Rows 53–58 Work in St st.
Row 59 K26, turn,. p12.
Cont in St st on center 12 sts only for 6 more rows to beg trunk.

TRUNK
Row 1 [K1, k2tog] 4 times—8 sts.
Row 2 P1, p2tog, p2, p2tog, p1—6 sts; turn and knit these 6 sts.
Row 3 Sl 6 sts back to LH needle, bring yarn around back and knit 6 sts.
Rep row 3 for 18 rows, creating I-cord. Bind off.
With RS facing, join yarn to rem sts from bottom of trunk and knit these 14 sts (which were not worked on row 59).
Row 60 P14, cast on 12 sts, purl to end—40 sts.
Rows 61–65 Work in St st.
Row 66 P11, k1, p16, k1, p11.
Row 67 K11, p1, k16, p1, k11.
Cont in pat for 3 more rows.
Row 71 [K2tog] across—20 sts.

Gauge
16 sts and 22 rows to 4"/10cm over St st using size 9 (5.5mm) needles.
Take time to check gauge.

Row 72 Purl.

Row 73 [K2tog] across—10 sts.

Cut yarn, leaving 12"/30.5cm tail. Thread tail through rem sts, pull tight and secure. Sew seam down to legs. Sew one leg completely closed. For second leg, sew the foot closed, leaving opening on the inside leg. Stuff the body lightly and evenly. Do not overstuff. Stuff the snout and sew to the side opening of the face.

Arm

Cast on 16 sts.

Rows 1–21 Work in St st, beg with a knit row.

Row 22 [P2tog] across—8 sts.

Cut yarn, leaving 12"/30.5cm tail. Thread tail through rem sts, pull tight and secure. Sew up the arm, stuff lightly, and stitch opening together. Sew arm onto body at shoulder level. Rep for second arm.

Right Ear

Cast on 5 sts.

Row 1 [Kfb] twice, knit to last 2 sts, [kfb] twice—9 sts.

Row 2 Purl.

Rows 3–6 Rep last two rows—17 sts.

Rows 7 and 8 Work in St st.

Row 9 [Kfb] twice, knit to last 2 sts, [kfb] twice—21 sts.

Rows 10–14 Work in St st.

Row 15 Knit to last 2 sts, [kfb] twice—23 sts.

Row 16 Purl.

Rows 17 and 18 Rep last two rows—25 sts.

Row 19 K2tog, knit to last 4 sts, [k2tog] twice—22 sts.

Row 20 Purl.

Rep rows 19 and 20 until 4 sts rem.

Next row [K2tog] twice—2 sts. Pass first st over second. Cut yarn, leaving 6"/15cm tail. Sew cast-on edge to purl bumps at side of head.

Left Ear

Work as for right ear through row 14.

Row 15 [Kfb] twice, knit to end—23 sts.

Row 16 Purl.

Rows 17 and 18 Rep rows 15 and 16—25 sts.

Row 19 [K2tog] twice, knit to last 2 sts, k2tog—22 sts.

Row 20 Purl.

Rep rows 19 and 20 until 4 sts rem.

Next row [K2tog] twice—2 sts. Pass first st over second. Cut yarn, leaving 6"/15cm tail. Sew cast-on edge to purl bumps at side of head.

Tail

Cast on 10 sts.

Bind off. Sew tail to the back seam on the bottom about 1"/2.5cm up from the legs.

Neck

Secure a 12"/30.5cm strand of yarn to base of head at back. With tapestry needle, weave in and out around base of head, pull tight and secure.

Finishing

Weave in ends. Prior to felting, thread several lengths of non-felting scrap yarn and run through the head, body, and legs of the piece, leaving long tails. This will hold the stuffing in place during felting. Be sure to run yarn from side-to-side and not through the front of the head, as "scars" can result from the yarn. Felt by machine as foll:

1) Use a low water setting and hottest temperature in a top-loading washing machine. Add small amount of laundry detergent and jeans or towels for agitation.

2) Place item in a lingerie bag or zippered pillowcase and add to machine. Check the felting progress frequently, removing item when the individual sts are no longer visible and item is felted to the desired size.

3) Place item in cool water to stop the felting process and remove suds. Remove from lingerie bag and roll gently in towel to remove excess water.

4) Block and shape while wet. Pat into shape, and allow to air dry completely.

When dry, finish eyes by needle felting with roving, referring to photo for placement. ∎

Graphic Mitts

These playful mitts combine a geometric pattern with a bright variegated background and pretty picot edging.

DESIGNED BY SHEILA JOYNES, DEBBIE MACOMBER'S A GOOD YARN SHOP, PORT ORCHARD, WA

◀■■■▢

Size
Woman's Medium

Knitted Measurements
Hand circumference 8"/20.5cm
Length 8¼"/21cm

Materials
■ 1 3½oz/100g hank (each approx 220yd/201m) of Cascade Yarns *Cascade 220 Paints* (wool) in #9859 tropical punch (MC)

■ 1 3½oz/100g hank (each approx 220yd/201m) of Cascade Yarns *Cascade 220* (wool) in #2413 red (CC)

■ One set (5) size 6 (3.75mm) double-pointed needles (dpns) *or size to obtain gauge*

■ Scrap yarn

■ Stitch markers

Mitts (make 2)
With MC, cast on 48 sts. Join to work in the rnd, being careful not to twist sts. Place marker (pm) for beg of rnd.
Rnds 2–7 *With MC, p2, with CC, k2; rep from * to end of rnd.
Rnd 8 With MC, k12, M1, k24, M1, k12—50 sts.
Beg working chart, pm every 10 sts to mark pat reps—5 total reps. Work through rnd 33.
Rnd 34 K 21 sts of chart pat, k next 8 sts (thumb sts) onto scrap yarn for thumb, return those 8 sts to LH needle, and cont in pat as est from chart.
Rnds 35–47 Work chart as est.

PICOT EDGING
Rnds 48–51 With MC, knit.
Rnd 52 *Yo, k2tog; rep from * to end of rnd.
Rnds 53–56 With MC, knit.
Bind off, fold picot edge to inside and sew in place.

Gauges
20 sts and 28 rows to 4"/10cm over St st using size 6 (3.75mm) needles.
26 sts and 31 rows to 4"/10cm over Fair Isle pat using size 6 (3.75mm) needles.
Take time to check gauges.

Graphic Mitts

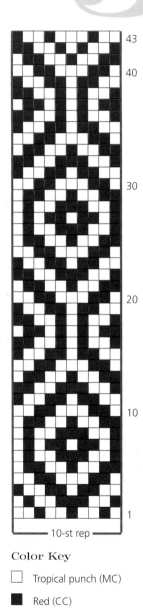

Color Key

☐ Tropical punch (MC)

■ Red (CC)

THUMB
Carefully remove waste yarn and place 8 sts below on your needle and 8 sts above on a dpn. Join MC and k8, pick up and k 1 st in gap, k8, pick up and k 1 st in gap, pm for beg of rnd—18 sts.
Rnds 1–3 Knit.
Rnd 4 K2tog, k14, k2tog—16 sts.
Rnds 5–6 Knit.
Rnd 7 Purl.
Rnd 8 Knit.
Rnd 9 Purl.
Bind off loosely.

Finishing

Sew up any remaining holes. Block lightly to measurements. ∎

Football Dog Sweater

Touchdown! Prepare your pup for the season with this adorable pigskin-shaped sweater.

DESIGNED BY CHERI CLARK, THE NAKED SHEEP KNIT SHOP, PORTLAND, OR

Sizes

Written for smallest size; three larger sizes are in parentheses. Smallest size is for a very small dog; largest size is for a medium-size dog. (See chest circumferences.)

Knitted Measurements

Chest circumference 10 (13, 16, 19)"/25.5 (33, 40.5, 40.5, 48)cm
Length Approx 10 (12, 14½, 16¾"/25.5 (30.5, 37, 42.5)cm

Materials

■ 1 3½oz/100g ball (each approx 220yd/201m) of Cascade Yarns *220 Superwash* (superwash wool) each in #823 burnt orange (MC) and #1961 camel (CC)

■ One each sizes 6 and 8 (4 and 5mm) circular needle, 16"/40cm long, *or size to obtain gauge*

■ Stitch holder

■ Size H/8 (5mm) crochet hook

■ Tapestry needle

■ Removable stitch markers

Stitch Glossary

M1R Insert LH needle from back to front under the strand between last st worked and next st on LH needle. K into the front loop to twist the st.
M1L Insert LH needle from front to back under the strand between last st worked and next st on LH needle. K into the back loop to twist the st.

K2, P2 Rib

(in rows, over multiple of 4 sts plus 2)
Row 1 (RS) *K2, p2; rep from * to last 2 sts, k2.
Row 2 (WS) *P2, k2; rep from * to last 2 sts, p2.
Rep rows 1 and 2 for k2, p2 rib in rows.

K2, P2 Rib

(in rnds, over multiple of 4 sts)
Rnd 1 *K2, p2; rep from * to end of rnd.
Rep rnd 1 for k2, p2 rib in rnds.

Sweater

With smaller needles and MC, cast on 38 (46, 54, 66) stitches, leaving 24"/61cm tail for seaming. Work in k2, p2 rib for 1 (1, 1¼, 1¼)"/2.5 (2.5, 3, 3)cm, ending with a WS row.
Change to CC and knit 4 rows. Place marker (pm) on a st in the middle of the 4th row of CC. Change to MC and larger needles.
Row 1 (RS) K2, M1R, k to last 2 stitches, M1L, k2.
Row 2 (WS) Purl.
Rep rows 1 and 2 until there are 46 (58, 72, 86) sts. Work even until piece measures 2 (2½, 3, 3½)"/5 (6.5, 7.5,

Gauge

18 sts and 24 rows to 4"/10cm over St st using size 8 (5mm) needles.
Take time to check gauge.

Football Dog Sweater

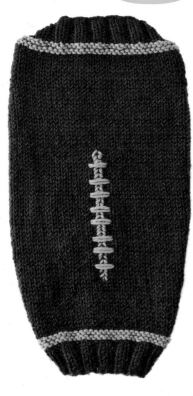

9)cm from marker, or desired length to leg opening, ending with a WS row.
Next row K5 (6, 7, 8), bind off 4 (5, 6, 7), k28 (36, 46, 56), bind off 4 (5, 6, 7), k5 (6, 7, 8).
Cont in St st, working each section separately, for 1 (1¼, 1½, 1¾)"/2.5 (3, 4, 4.5)cm from leg bind-off, ending with WS row.
Next row Rejoin sections as foll: K5 (6, 7, 8), cast on 4 (5, 6, 7), k28 (36, 46, 56), cast on 4 (5, 6, 7), k5 (6, 7, 8).
Cont in St st as est until piece measures 4½ (5½, 6½, 7½)"/11.5 (14, 16.5, 19)cm from marker, ending with a WS row. Bind off 4 (6, 8, 10) stitches at beg of next 2 rows.

Next row K1, k2tog, k to last 3 sts, ssk, k1.
Next row Purl.
Rep last 2 rows until 24 (30, 36, 42) sts rem. Cont in St st as est until piece measures 7 (9, 11, 13)"/18 (23, 28, 33)cm from marker, or 1"/2.5cm less than desired length of sweater. Cut yarn and place rem sts on holder.
Using tail from cast-on edge, seam bottom of sweater together.
Beg at seam and using smaller needle and CC, pick up and k every stitch along flat underside shaping; pick up and k 3 out of every 4 sts along first side of sweater; k all sts on holder; pick up and k 3 out of every 4 sts along second side of sweater; and pick up and k every stitch remaining along flat underside shaping, end with multiple of 4 sts. Pm for beg of rnd.
Next rnd Purl.
Next rnd Knit.
Next rnd Purl.
Change to MC and knit one rnd. Work in k2, p2 rib for 1"/2.5cm. Bind off in rib.

Finishing
Block lightly to measurements. Using CC, single crochet around the leg openings for a finished edge.

LACES
With CC, create the laces using duplicate st, beg approx 1½ (1½, 2, 2)"/ 4 (4, 5, 5)cm down from marker. Long strip should measure approx 4 (4, 5, 5)"/ 10 (10, 12.5, 12.5)cm long, with 6–8 short strips crossing it. Refer to photo for placement. ▮

Slip Stitch Hat

A two-color slip stitch pattern that evokes brickwork is simple to knit but makes a big impact.

DESIGNED BY LESLIE ROTH, THE KNITTING STUDIO, MONTPELIER, VT

Sizes

Instructions are written for Adult Small. Changes for Medium, Large, and X-Large are in parentheses.

Knitted Measurements

Brim circumference (slightly stretched)
18½ (20, 21½, 23)"/47 (51, 55, 58.5)cm

Materials

■ 1 3½oz/100g ball (each approx 220yd/201m) of Cascade Yarns *220 Superwash* (superwash wool) each in #856 aporto (A) and #810 teal (B)

■ One each sizes 5 and 6 (3.75 and 4mm) circular needle, 16"/41cm long, *or size to obtain gauge*

■ One set (5) size 6 (4mm) double-pointed needles (dpns)

■ Tapestry needle

Slip Stitch Pattern

Rnds 1 and 2 With A, knit.
Rnds 3 and 4 With B, k1, *sl 1 wyib, k3; rep from * to last 3 sts, sl 1 wyib, k2.
Rnds 5 and 6 With A, knit.
Rnds 7 and 8 With B, k3, *sl 1 wyib, k3; rep from * to last st, sl 1.
Rep rnds 1–8 for sl st pat.

K2, P2 Rib

(multiple of 4 sts)
Rnd 1 *K2, p2, rep from * to end of rnd.
Rep rnd 1 for k2, p2 rib.

Hat

Using smaller needles and A, cast on 96 (104, 112, 120) sts. Join, being careful not to twist sts, and place marker for beg of rnd.
Work in k2, p2 rib for 1 (1, 1½, 1½)"/2.5 (2.5, 4, 4)cm.
Work rnds 1–8 of sl st pat a total of 4 (4, 5, 5) times.
With A, knit 2 rnds.

CROWN SHAPING

Note Change to dpns when sts no longer comfortably fit on circular needle.
Rnd 1 *K2tog, k6; rep from * to end of rnd.
Rnd 2 and all even-numbered rnds Knit.
Rnd 3 *K2tog, k5; rep from * to end of rnd.
Rnd 5 *K2tog, k4; rep from * to end of rnd.
Rnd 7 *K2tog, k3; rep from * to end of rnd.
Rnd 9 *K2tog, k2; rep from * to end of rnd.
Rnd 11 *K2tog, k1; rep from * to end of rnd.
Rnd 13 K2tog to end of rnd.
Rnd 15 K2tog to end of rnd.
Break yarn, leaving an 8"/20.5cm tail. Thread through rem sts. Pull tog tightly and secure end.

Finishing

Block lightly to measurements. ■

Gauges

20 sts and 24 rows to 4"/10cm over St st using size 6 (4mm) needles.
21 sts and 24 rows to 4"/10cm over sl st pat using size 6 (4mm) needles.
Take time to check gauges.

Two-Color Lace Cap

A simple lace pattern and contrasting brim add a touch of flair to a pretty pastel baby hat.

DESIGNED BY AIMEE OSUCH, AIMEE'S YARN CAFE, PARADISE, CA

■■□□

Size
Newborn to 3 months

Knitted Measurements
Brim circumference 12"/30.5cm

Materials
■ 1 3½oz/100g ball (each approx 220yd/201m) of Cascade Yarns *220 Superwash* (superwash wool) each in #1915 banana, #1942 mint, #840 iris, and #894 strawberry cream

■ Size 7 (4.5mm) circular needle, 16"/40cm long, *or size to obtain gauge*

■ One set (5) size 7 (4.5mm) double-pointed needles (dpns)

■ Stitch marker

■ Tapestry needle

Notes
1) Mix and match colors, using any two as MC and CC.
2) Change to dpns when sts no longer comfortably fit on circular needle.

Cap
With circular needles and CC, cast on 48 sts. Join to work in the rnd, being careful not to twist sts, and place marker (pm) for beg of rnd.
Work in St st (knit every rnd) for 6 rnds. Change to MC and knit 2 rnds.

BEG LACE PAT
Rnd 1 *Yo, sl 1, k1, psso, k10; rep from * to end of rnd.
Rnd 2 and all even-numbered rnds Knit.
Rnd 3 *K1, yo, sl 1, k1, psso, k7, k2tog, yo; rep from * to end of rnd.
Rnd 5 *K2, yo, sl 1, k1, psso, k5, k2tog, yo, k1; rep from * to end of rnd.
Rnd 7 *K3, yo, sl 1, k1, psso, k3, k2tog, yo, k2; rep from * to end of rnd.
Rnd 9 *K6, yo, sl 1, k1, psso, k4; rep from * to end of rnd.
Rnd 11 *K4, k2tog, yo, k1, yo, sl 1, k1, psso, k3; rep from * to end of rnd.

Gauge
17 sts and 24 rows to 4"/10cm over St st using size 7 (4.5mm) needles.
Take time to check gauge.

Two-Color Lace Cap

56

Rnd 13 *K3, k2tog, yo, k3, yo, sl 1, k1, psso, k2; rep from * to end of rnd.
Rnd 15 *K2, k2tog, yo, k5, yo, sl 1, k1, psso, k1; rep from * to end of rnd.
Rep rnds 1–5 once more.

CROWN SHAPING
Rnd 1 K3, sl 1, k1, psso, k3, k2tog, *k5, sl 1, k1, psso, k3, k2tog; rep from * to last 2 sts, k2—40 sts.
Rnd 2 K1, k2tog, yo, k1, sl 1, k2tog, psso, k1, *yo, sl 1, k1, psso, k1, k2tog, yo, k1, sl 1, k2tog, psso, k1; rep from * to last 2 sts, yo, sl 1, k1, psso—32 sts.
Rnd 3 K2, k2tog, *k1, sl 1, k1, psso, k3, k2tog; rep from * to last 4 sts, k1, sl 1, k1, psso, k1—24 sts.
Rnd 4 *K4, k2tog; rep from * to end of rnd—20 sts.
Rnd 5 *K3, k2tog; rep from * to end of rnd—16 sts.
Rnd 6 *K2, k2tog; rep from * to end of rnd—12 sts.
Rnd 7 *K1, k2tog; rep from * to end of rnd—8 sts.
Rnd 8 K2tog to end of rnd—4 sts.
Break yarn, leaving 6"/15cm tail. Thread through rem sts and pull tightly to secure.

Finishing
Block lightly to measurements. ◼

57

Shell Lace Shawlette

A shawl knit with fingering-weight yarn and a delicate shell lace edging is petite and pretty.

DESIGNED BY KRISTEN ASHBAUGH HELMREICH, JIMMY BEANS WOOL, RENO, NV

Knitted Measurements
Width at top 80"/203cm
Height at center 18"/45.5cm

Materials
■ 3 1¾oz/50g hanks (each approx 273yd/250m) of Cascade Yarns *Cascade 220 Fingering* (wool) in #8908 anis

■ One pair size 4 (3.5mm) needles *or size to obtain gauge*

■ Size 6 (3.5mm) circular needle, 32"/81cm long

Shell Lace Pattern
(multiple of 13 sts)
Row 1 *K2tog, k9, ssk; rep from * to end.
Row 2 Purl.
Row 3 *K2tog, k7, ssk; rep from * to end.
Row 4 Purl.
Row 5 *K2tog, yo, [k1, yo] 5 times, ssk; rep from * to end.
Row 6 Knit.
Rep rnds 1–6 for shell lace pat.

Gauge
26 sts and 48 rows to 4"/10cm over garter st (k every row) using size 4 (3.5mm) needles.
Take time to check gauge.

Shell Lace Shawlette

Shawlette
With straight needles, make a slip knot and place it on your needle. K1 into the slip knot.
Row 1 Yo, k1.
Row 2 K2.
Row 3 Yo, k2.
Row 4 K3.
Row 5 Yo, k3.
Row 6 K4.

BEG INCREASES
Row 1 *Yo, k1, k2tog, k; rep from * to end.
Row 2 Knit.
Row 3 *Yo, k1; rep from * to end.
Row 4 Knit.
Rep rows 1–4 until piece measures 35"/89cm, end with row 4.
Work even for 3"/7.5cm more as foll:
Row 1 *Yo, k1, k2tog, k; rep from * to end of row.
Row 2 Knit.
Rep rows 1 and 2 until piece measures 38"/96.5cm, end with row 2.

BEG DECREASES
Row 1 *Yo, k1, k2tog, k; rep from * to end.
Row 2 Knit to last 4 sts, k2tog, k2.
Row 3 *Yo, k1, k2tog, k; rep from * to end.
Row 4 Knit.
Rep rows 1–4 until 4 sts rem, end with row 4.

SHAPE END
Row 1 Yo, k1, k2tog, k1.
Row 2 K1, k2tog, k1.
Row 3 Yo, k2tog, k1.
Row 4 K2tog, k1.
Row 5 Yo, k2tog.
Row 6 K2tog.
Break yarn and pull strand through the rem lp.

LACE EDGING
With circular needle, pick up and k 1 st in each yo along edge of shawl—355 sts total.
Row 1 Knit.
Row 2 Knit, inc 26 sts evenly across—377 sts.
Rows 3–8 Knit.
Work rows 1–6 of shell lace pat 3 times.
Bind off.

Finishing
Block lightly to measurements, pinning out each point along the lace edge. ■

Mitered Squares Cardi

Mitered squares on the body and stripes on the sleeves add up to an adorable first cardi.

DESIGNED BY LISA CARNEY DOHERTY, COZY, DURHAM, NC

■■■▢

Size
Infant to 12 months

Knitted Measurements
Chest 21"/53.5cm
Length 10"/25.5cm

Materials
■ 2 3½oz/100g balls (each approx 220yd/201m) of Cascade Yarns *220 Superwash* (superwash wool) in #834 strawberry pink (A)
■ 1 ball in #1941 salmon (B)
■ One pair size 6 (4mm) needles *or size to obtain gauge*
■ Size 6 (4mm) circular needle, 24"/60cm long
■ One size G/6 (4mm) crochet hook
■ Stitch markers
■ Three buttons, ¾"/19mm diameter

Stripe Pattern
Working in garter st throughout, *knit 2 rows with B, 2 rows with A; rep from * for stripe pat.

Notes
1) Slip 1 st at beg of every row purlwise.
2) Left back and front of cardigan body are worked in horizontal rows of squares.
3) Right back and front of cardigan body are worked in vertical rows of squares.
4) Use assembly diagram as a guide, matching squares.
5) Sleeves are worked from armhole edge down to cuff and then set into armhole opening.

Left Back/Front
FIRST ROW OF SQUARES
Square 1
Row 1 (RS) With straight needles and A, cast on 25 sts.
Row 2 K24, p1.
Row 3 With B, sl 1, k10, SK2P, k10, p1—23 sts.
Row 4 With B, sl 1, knit to last st, p1.
Row 5 With A, sl 1, k9, SK2P, k9, p1—21 sts.
Row 6 With A, sl 1, knit to last st, p1.

Row 7 With B, sl 1, k8, p1—19 sts.
Row 8 With B, sl 1, knit to last st, p1.
Row 9 With A, sl 1, k7, SK2P, k7, p1—17 sts.
Row 10 With A, sl 1, knit to last st, p1.
Row 11 With B, sl 1, k6, SK2P, k6, p1—15 sts.
Row 12 With B, sl 1, knit to last st, p1.
Cont in pat as est, working 1 less st either side of center SK2P and alternating colors every 2 rows, until 3 sts rem.
Next row (RS) With A, SK2P—1 st.
Do not break yarns.
Square 2 Turn last completed square 90 degrees clockwise and, with RS facing and A, pick up and k 12 sts along side edge of last completed square, turn work and cast on 12 sts—25 sts. Starting with row 2, work as for square 1—1 st.
Square 3 Work as for square 2.
Square 4 Work as for square 2—1 st. Bind off.

SECOND ROW OF SQUARES
Square 5 With straight needles and A, cast on 12 sts, pick up and k 13 sts along top edge of square 1—25 sts. Starting with row 2, work as for square 1—1 st.

Gauges
20 sts and 40 rows to 4"/10cm over garter st using size 6 (4mm) needles.
One square measures 2¾"/7cm x 2¾"/7cm.
Take time to check gauges.

Mitered Squares Cardi

58

Square 6 Turn work 90 degrees clockwise and, with RS facing and A,
pick up and k 11 sts along side edge of square 5, pick up and k 1 corner st, turn work and pick up and k 12 sts along top edge of square 2—25 sts. Starting with row 2, work as for square 1—1 st.

Square 7 Turn work 90 degrees clockwise and, with RS facing and A, pick up and k 11 sts along side edge of square 6, pick up and k 1 corner st, turn work and pick up and k 12 sts along top edge of square 3—25 sts. Starting with row 2, work as for square 1—1 st.

Square 8 Turn work 90 degrees clockwise and, with RS facing and A, pick up and k 11 sts along side edge of square 7, pick up and k 1 corner st, turn work and pick up and k 12 sts along top edge of square 4—25 sts. Starting with row 2, work as for square 1—1 st. Fasten off.

THIRD ROW OF SQUARES

Square 9 With straight needles and A, cast on 12 sts, pick up and k 13 sts along top edge of square 5—25 sts. Starting with row 2, work as for square 1—1 st.

Square 10 Turn work 90 degrees clockwise and, with RS facing and A, pick up and k 11 sts along side edge of square 9, pick up and k 1 corner st, turn work and pick up and k 12 sts along top edge of square 6—25 sts. Starting with row 2, work as for square 1—1 st. Fasten off.

LEFT ARMHOLE OPENING

Square 11 With straight needles and A, cast on 12 sts, pick up and k 13 sts along top edge of square 7—25 sts. Starting with row 2, work as for square 1—1 st.

NECK SHAPING

Triangle 12 Turn work 90 degrees clockwise and, with RS facing and A, pick up and k 11 sts along side edge of square 11, pick up and k 1 corner st, turn work and pick up and k 12 sts along top edge of square 8—25 sts.

Row 1 (WS) With B, sl 1, k23, p1.
Row 2 With B, sl 1, ssk, k8, SK2P, k8, k2tog, p1—21 sts.
Row 3 With B, sl 1, knit to last st, p1.
Row 4 With A, sl 1, ssk, k6, SK2P, k6, k2tog, p1—17 sts.
Row 5 With A, sl 1, knit to last st, p1.
Row 6 With B, sl 1, ssk, k4, SK2P, k4, k2tog, p1—13 sts.
Row 7 With B, sl 1, knit to last st, p1.
Row 8 With A, sl 1, ssk, k2, SK2P, k2, k2tog, p1—9 sts.
Row 9 With A, sl 1, knit to last st, p1.
Row 10 With B, sl 1, ssk, SK2P, k2tog, p1—5 sts.
Row 11 With B, sl 1, k3, p1.
Row 12 With B, sl 2 sts, k3tog, pass both slipped sts over—1 st. Fasten off.

FOURTH ROW OF SQUARES

Square 13 With straight needles and A, cast on 12 sts, pick up and k 13 sts along top edge of square 9—25 sts. Starting with row 2, work as for square 1—1 st.

Square 14 Turn work 90 degrees clockwise and, with RS facing and A, pick up and k 11 sts along side edge of square 13, pick up and k 1 corner st, turn work and pick up and k 12 sts along top edge of square 10—25 sts. Starting with row 2, work as for square 1—1 st. Fasten off.

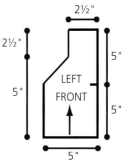

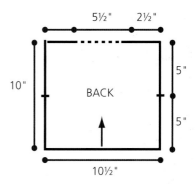

Mitered Squares Cardi

LEFT ARMHOLE OPENING

Square 15 With straight needles and A, cast on 12 sts, pick up and k 13 sts along top edge of square 11—25 sts. Starting with row 2, work as for square 1—1 st. Fasten off.

Right Back/Front

FIRST ROW OF SQUARES

Square 16 With straight needles and A, cast on 12 sts, pick up and k 13 sts along side edge of square 1—25 sts. Starting with row 2, work as for square 1—1 st.

Square 17 With RS facing and A, pick up and k 11 sts along top edge of square 16, pick up and k 1 corner st, turn work and pick up and k 12 sts along side edge of square 5—25 sts. Starting with row 2, work as for square 1—1 st.

Square 18 With RS facing and A, pick up and k 11 sts along top edge of square 17, pick up and k 1 corner st, turn work and pick up and k 12 sts along side edge of square 9—25 sts. Starting with row 2, work as for square 1—1 st.

Square 19 With RS facing and A, pick up and k 11 sts along top edge of square 18, pick up and k 1 corner st, turn work and pick up and k 12 sts along side edge of square 13—25 sts. Starting with row 2, work as for square 1—1 st. Fasten off.

SECOND ROW OF SQUARES

Square 20 With straight needles and A, cast on 12 sts, pick up and k 13 sts along side edge of square 16—25 sts. Starting with row 2, work as for square 1—1 st.

Square 21 With RS facing and A, pick up and k 11 sts along top edge of square 20, pick up and k 1 corner st, turn work and pick up and k 12 sts along side edge of square 17—25 sts. Starting with row 2, work as for square 1—1 st.

Square 22 With RS facing and A, pick up and k 11 sts along top edge of square 20, pick up and k 1 corner st, turn work and pick up and k 12 sts along side edge of square 18—25 sts. Starting with row 2, work as for square 1—1 st.

Square 23 With RS facing and A, pick up and k 11 sts along top edge of square 22, pick up and k 1 corner st, turn work and pick up and k 12 sts along side edge of square 19—25 sts. Starting with row 2, work as for square 1—1 st. Fasten off.

THIRD ROW OF SQUARES

Square 24 With straight needles and A, cast on 12 sts, pick up and k 13 sts along side edge of square 20—25 sts. Starting with row 2, work as for square 1—1 st.

Square 25 With RS facing and A, pick up and k 11 sts along top edge of square 24, pick up and k 1 corner st, turn work and pick up and k 12 sts along side edge of square 21—25 sts. Starting with row 2, work as for square 1—1 st. Fasten off.

RIGHT ARMHOLE OPENING

Square 26 With RS facing and A, pick up and k 11 sts along top edge of square 25, pick up and k 1 corner st, cast on 12 sts—25 sts. Starting with row 2, work as for square 1—1 st.

Square 27 With RS facing and A, pick up and k 11 sts along top edge of square 27, pick up and k 1 corner st, cast on 12 sts—25 sts. Starting with row 2, work as for square 1—1 st. Fasten off.

FOURTH ROW OF SQUARES

Square 28 With straight needles and A, cast on 12 sts, pick up and k 13 sts along side edge of square 24—25 sts. Starting with row 2, work as for square 1—1 st.

Square 29 With RS facing and A, pick up and k 11 sts along top edge of square 28, pick up and k 1 corner st, turn work and pick up and k 12 sts along side edge of square 25—25 sts. Starting with row 2, work as for square 1—1 st.

NECK SHAPING

Triangle 30 With RS facing and A, pick up and k 11 sts along top edge of square 29, pick up and k 1 corner st, turn work and pick up and k 12 sts along side edge of square 26—25 sts.

Row 2 (WS) With A, sl 1, k23, p1.
Row 3 With B, sl 1, ssk, k8, SK2P, k8, k2tog, p1—21 sts.
Row 4 With B, sl 1, knit to last st, p1.
Row 5 With A, sl 1, ssk, k6, SK2P, k6, k2tog, p1—17 sts.
Row 6 With A, sl 1, knit to last st, p1.
Row 7 With B, sl 1, ssk, k4, SK2P, k4, k2tog, p1—13 sts.
Row 8 With B, sl 1, knit to last st, p1.
Row 9 With A, sl 1, ssk, k2, SK2P, k2, k2tog, p1—9 sts.
Row 10 With A, sl 1, knit to last st, p1.
Row 11 With B, sl 1, ssk, SK2P, k2tog, p1—5 sts.
Row 12 With B, sl 1, k3, p1.
Row 13 With B, sl 2 sts, k3tog, pass both slipped sts over—1 st. Fasten off.

Sleeves

With straight needles and B, cast on 52 sts. Working in garter st following stripe pat, dec 1 st at each end of 11th and every following 6th row 6 times more—36 sts.
Work even in stripe pat until piece measures 6"/15cm, ending with 2 rows A.
Next row (RS) With A, k3, k2tog, [k5, k2tog] 4 times, k3—31 sts.
Next row With A, knit.
Next row With A, purl.
Next row With A, knit. Bind off all sts purlwise.

ASSEMBLY DIAGRAM

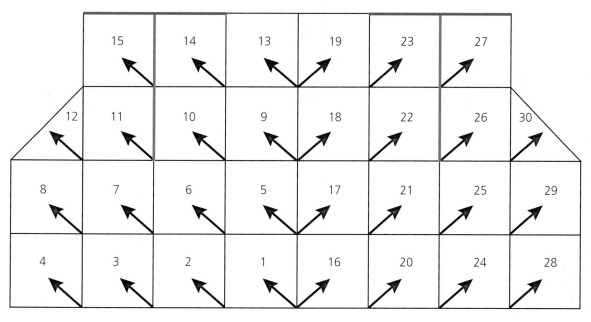

15	14	13	19	23	27
12	11	10	9	18	22	26	30
8	7	6	5	17	21	25	29
4	3	2	1	16	20	24	28

Key

━━ Armhole openings   ━━ Shoulder seams

Finishing

Sew sleeve seam. Sew sleeves into armhole openings.
Sew top edges of squares 14 and 15 tog for left shoulder seam. Rep for right shoulder seam, using squares 23 and 27.

EDGING

With circular needle, RS facing and A, starting at center back neck, pick up and k 12 sts evenly along outer edge of square 13, place marker (pm), pick up and k 1 st at corner, turn work and pick up and k 12 sts evenly along outer edge of square 15 and triangle 12, turn work and pick up and k 12 sts evenly along outer edge of squares 8 and 4, pm, pick up and k 1 st at corner, turn work and pick up and k 12 sts evenly along lower edge of squares 4, 3, 2, 1, 16, 20, 24, and 28, pm, turn work and pick up and k 1 st at corner, turn work and pick up and k 12 sts evenly along outer edge of

squares 28 and 29, turn work and pick up and k 12 sts evenly along outer edge of triangle 30 and square 27, pm, pick up and k 1 st at corner, turn work and pick up and k 12 sts evenly along outer edge of square 19—220 sts.
Join and pm for beg of rnd.
Rnd 1 Purl.
Rnd 2 Purl to first marker, M1, sl marker, p1, M1, *purl to next marker, M1, sl marker, p1, M1; rep from * twice more, purl to end of rnd—228 sts.
Rnd 3 Purl.
Bind off all sts purlways.
Using photo as a guide, sew 3 buttons to left front edging.

BUTTON LOOPS (MAKE 3)

With crochet hook and A, join with a slip st to bound-off row of cardigan edging, opposite button. Ch 7. Sl st into same space as first sl st. Fasten off. ■

171

59

Mesh Cowl

A simple-to-knit openwork pattern adds textural interest to a cowl that can be wrapped twice for extra warmth.

DESIGNED BY SARAH BASS, DANCING GOAT YARN SHOP, WARSAW, NY

◖■☐☐

Knitted Measurements
Circumference 48"/122cm
Width 7"/18cm

Materials
▦ 2 3½oz/100g hanks (each approx 220yd/201m) of Cascade Yarns *Cascade 220 Heathers* (wool) in #2423 Montmartre

▦ Size 8 (5mm) circular needle, 32"/80cm long, *or size to obtain gauge*

▦ Stitch marker

Mesh Pattern
(multiple of 2 sts)
Rnd 1 Purl.
Rnd 2 *Sl 1 purlwise wyib, k1; rep from * around.
Rnd 3 *Sl 1 purlwise wyib, p1; rep from * around.
Rnd 4 *Yo, k2tog; rep from * around.
Rnd 5 Purl.
Rep rnds 1–5 for mesh pat.

Cowl
Cast on 200 sts. Join to work in the rnd, taking care not to twist sts, and place marker for beg of rnd.
Rnds 1–7 Knit.
Rnds 8–12 Work rnds 1–5 of mesh pat.
Rnds 13–18 Knit.
Rnds 19–23 Work rnds 1–5 of mesh pat.
Rnds 24 and 25 Knit.
Rnds 26–30 Work rnds 1–5 of mesh pat.
Rnds 31 and 32 Knit.
Rnds 33–37 Work rnds 1–5 of mesh pat.
Rnds 38–42 Knit.
Rnds 43–47 Work rnds 1–5 of mesh pat.
Rnds 48–54 Knit.
Bind off.

Finishing
Block lightly to measurements. ■

Gauge
18 sts and 28 rnds to 4"/10cm over mesh pat using size 8 (5mm) needles.
Take time to check gauge.

60

Ruffled Garter Capelet

A ruffled edge and a beautiful colorway make an easy garter-stitch knit look impressively luxurious.

DESIGNED BY CARLA BAKER-GIURFA, ELEMENTAL YARNS, SHOREWOOD, IL

Knitted Measurements
Width at top edge Approx 26"/66cm
Width at bottom edge Approx 80"/203cm
Height (including ruffle) Approx 12½"/32cm

Materials
■ 3 3½oz/100g balls (each approx 220yd/201m) of Cascade Yarns *220 Superwash Paints* in #9997 juniper berries
■ Size 9 (5.5mm) circular needle, 40"/101cm long, *or size to obtain gauge*
■ Removable stitch markers

Capelet
Cast on 80 sts.
Rows 1–6 Knit.
Row 7 (RS) *Kfb, k1; rep from * to end—120 sts.
Rows 8–18 Knit.
Row 19 *Kfb, k1; rep from * to end—180 sts.
Rows 20–34 Knit.
Row 35 *Kfb, k1: rep from * to end—270 sts.
Rows 36–38 Knit.
Place marker at each end of row for ruffle edge.

EDGE SHAPING
Next (dec) row K2tog, k to last 2 sts, ssk—268 sts. Knit 1 row.
Rep last 2 rows once more—266 sts.
Then rep dec row every row until 204 sts rem.
Next row (dec) [K2tog] twice, k to last 4 sts, [ssk] twice—200 sts.
Rep last row every row until 180 sts rem. Bind off.

RUFFLE EDGING
With RS facing, and starting at 1st marker, pick up and k 268 sts evenly across lower edge to 2nd marker.
Inc row (WS) Kfb in each st across—536 sts.
Starting with a RS row, work in St st for 1"/2.5cm, ending with a RS row. With WS facing, bind off knitwise.

Finishing
Block lightly to measurements. ■

Gauge
18 sts and 34 rows to 4"/10cm over garter st using size 9 (5.5mm) needles.
Take time to check gauge.

index

Vase on cover courtesy of
Alyssa Ettinger Design
www.alyssaettinger.com